THE EMPTY QUIVER

A Journey from the Pain of Despair and Loss to Recovery, Hope and Victory

Dr. Anthony Walton

THE EMPTY QUIVER
Copyright © 2017 by Walton Publishing

All rights reserved. No part of this book may be reproduced or transmitted in any form or by any means without written permission from the author.

ISBN 978-0-692-90073-4

Walton Publishing
Indianapolis, Indiana

Printed in USA

waltonpublishing@sbcglobal.net

Dedication

I dedicate this book to my deceased mother, Ethel Curry Walton, who was always there as a source of support, often giving advice even during times when it was not fully appreciated. A woman who prayed for me when I wanted to go my own way, who saw the good in me when no one else could. A woman who always told me that I could accomplish whatever I wanted and encouraged me to believe in myself at times when I was not sure of my purpose.

To my deceased siblings, my brother James and my baby sister, Debra Walton; who I was very close to and miss our special times together.

To the great men, who were not in the ministry, but in the absence of a father had a tremendous influence in my life: my grandfather, Thomas Curry, who I admired and respected; my uncle, Clarence Curry, who would often give me instructions as a young man when I was unsure of myself; Edward Trammel, Sr. who would often correct me with a firm hand and tell me, "You don't have to be like these other young men, not doing anything for themselves, but be the best you can be"; Fred Morris, who taught me to be a photographer and was never hesitant to correct me when he felt I may have been going astray.

Finally, to all my family and friends who were not mentioned by name, your impact in my life has been immeasurable and will always be appreciated.

TABLE OF CONTENTS

Acknowledgements vii
Forewords ix
CHAPTER 1:   The Purpose 1
CHAPTER 2:   The Question of When or How Many 4
CHAPTER 3:   Infertility/Barrenness 9
CHAPTER 4:   What is the Problem? The Test! 11
CHAPTER 5:   She Wants to Have My Baby but
                              She's Not My Wife 18
CHAPTER 6:   I'm Pregnant 22
CHAPTER 7:   The Early Labor 24
CHAPTER 8:   The Phone Call 30
CHAPTER 9:   The Death/Funeral/Returning Baby Furniture 34
CHAPTER 10: Will Love Keep Us Together? 37
CHAPTER 11: The Question to God, "Why?" 41
CHAPTER 12: The Anger and the Loss of Desire to Pray 43
Why is it Necessary to Pray? 51
CHAPTER 13: The Desire to be Left Alone 52
CHAPTER 14: The Baby Shower 54
CHAPTER 15: Insensitivity from Others 56
Going Back to Work (More Insensitivity) 57
CHAPTER 16: The Grief/Anniversaries/Birth-Death 60
*Seven Stages of Grief – Through the Process
and Back to Life* 63
CHAPTER 17: The Accepting of God's Will 64
CHAPTER 18: Should We Try Again to Have Another Child?
                              69
CHAPTER 19: I'm Pregnant Again 72

CHAPTER 20: Thought for Pastors on Mother's
    Day/Father's Day 76
CHAPTER 21: It's a Girl! 78
CHAPTER 22: Making It to Thirty-Two Weeks 80
CHAPTER 23: The Day Before the Delivery 84
CHAPTER 24: The Day of the Delivery 85
Taking Extra Precautions 85
CHAPTER 25: She's Here! 87
CHAPTER 26: The Sharing of Your Loss with Others 91
CHAPTER 27: The Little Red Wagon 95
CHAPTER 28: You Are Not Alone! 97
References 100
About the Author 104

Acknowledgements

To my lovely wife, Shirley Walton, for without you, I would not have been able to write this book. You have been a support and source of encouragement throughout this process. We have grown together and you have been there for me when no one else was there. You have been my sounding board, my encourager, and often a silent source of strength for me, as well as many others.

Thanks to my sisters, Elmira Walton and Brenda Morris, who always encouraged me to do my best and showed concern and support for whatever I have attempted to achieve. I am also grateful for friends and family who have been there throughout the years as support.

To Uz and Mary Tinker for raising my wife from the age of ten years, after the death of her parents, and instructing and assisting her in becoming the beautiful woman and wife she is today.

To those in the ministry, including Bishop James E. Tyson, Bishop Morris E. Golder, Bishop Benjamin T. Moore, Bishop Michael Shelby, and Bishop Byron Johnson, who have imparted their wisdom into my life.

To my editor, Heather Fox, for her assistance and tireless commitment.

Foreword

The material found in this book reveals the true feelings of two people wanting what is considered normal for married people. However, the frustrations and realities shared by the author open the door for a level of knowledge, information, compassion and reality that could assist anyone facing like situations.

As I read, the anticipation felt by the couple leading up to the test to discovering the problem they faced, I was intrigued to reach the next line to see and feel, along with them, what was ahead.

I would not hesitate to say, if you have a child, or children, or know of anyone that has suffered a loss, you are certain to find this material stimulating and revelatory. Your anticipation for what happens next is sure to grip your heart. The raw sharing of their true feelings bleed through with a plain sense of reality, which is sure to at least temporarily place you in their shoes.

If you should wonder why anyone would, or should, share such private and painful information, I would say, the one who cried yesterday gained a measure of knowledge to know how to dry the tears of those who cry today.

I can see the value of this book being used in premarital classes and counseling sessions by a compassionate leader. You will notice that Bishop Walton did not hide his true feelings, before the testing of their bodies and the offers he encountered to plant his seeds in the wrong field. One can sense the vulnerable positions that infertility could present.

The reading of the Walton's' story is sure to make one more sensitive about childless couples and better equips us with insight that could help others cope with the empty feeling of incompleteness.

I can only wish and hope that you, the reader, will find the level of realness I discovered while reading. If you do, you are sure to tell others how rewarding it would be for them to read this book.

Bishop Clifton Jones
Pentecostal Assemblies of the World
Diocese of Mississippi and Western Kentucky

Foreword

Having spent more than forty years in ministry as a pastor and Bishop of an International church and along with being the natural father of seven children and a host of grandchildren, I have witnessed many Christians who have experienced the heartbreaking pains of both the death of a child as well as those who, for various reasons, have suffered with the inability to birth a child. In this book, *The Empty Quiver*, Bishop Anthony Walton takes us on a journey from the pains of despair and loss to recovery, hope and victory.

The Bible commands that we should be able to communicate our faith, 1 Peter 3:15, "But in your hearts set apart Christ as Lord. Always be prepared to give an answer to everyone who asks you to give the reason for the hope that you have. But do this with gentleness and respect."

The Apostle Paul demonstrates this to us in Acts 26. When he stood before King Agrippa, he told him logically and clearly, about his life before salvation, how he came to know Christ, and the life transforming change it made in his life. This same willingness to share with us, the readers, his challenges, his faith, his struggles and determination to stay committed to his beliefs, in the face of adversity, is like that of Paul's.

As a victorious overcomer of life's most difficult challenges, a dynamic speaker, motivator, and powerful minister, the author of this book has a life-changing message that others need to hear.

Bishop G. F. Austin, Diocesan
Pentecostal Assemblies of the World
Diocese of Alabama

Chapter 1
THE PURPOSE

The purpose of writing this book is to share with the readers the challenges, heartaches, and pains of those desiring to have a child, as well as those who have suffered the devastating loss of a child. I will not only discuss the effects it has on the couples who have suffered the loss, but also the effects it can have on the immediate family, friends, community and all those who are close to the family.

One of the questions I searched out as I began my research concerning this very touching subject was, as I previously mentioned, just how many people are affected and to what degree does the loss of a child or the inability to have a child affect the faith of those involved. Will this heartbreaking experience of pain and hurt strengthen the family unit, or will it be enough to completely destroy their relationship?

According to the Center for Disease Control and Prevention, 3,999,386 infants were born in the United States in 2010, 3% less than in 2009. The number of births fell for nearly all race and Hispanic origin groups. The birth rate in 2010 was 13.0 per 1,000 people.

When we look at these numbers many of those who have been fortunate enough to bear children, without any problems, may consider them and think nothing of it. But for those who are unable to have a child, and wished that they could, it leads them to question, "Why are so many children born each year and why have I/we not been able to have a child?"

I would like to carry the readers on a personal journey with my wife and myself, as we were one of the ones who found ourselves asking the question, "Why aren't we able to have a child?" I will be quite honest with my feelings and our personal struggles throughout our journey as we attempted to have a child, as well as during the loss of our son. My heart goes out to all those men and women, husband and wives who have attempted unsuccessfully to have a child, or have suffered the loss of a child. My wife and I are very well able to empathize with your journey of ups and downs, highs, lows, and disappointments.

"As arrows are in the hand of a warrior,
so are the children of one's youth."
(*Psalms 127:4, Amplified Bible*)

In the article "Crafting God's Arrows", Dennis and Barbara Rainey refer to Psalms 127:3-5. They make a comparison of arrows in the hands of the warrior. They speak of the relationship of children to that of arrows in the warrior's sheath or quiver, as well as the various aspects of these arrows. For example, they talk about the arrow's shaft as "identity", its feathers as "character", its nock as "relationships", and its point as a "mission" (Rainey, 1998).

When we think of arrows in a quiver, we normally do not think of them as children. We think of them as necessary tools for the warrior to use to hunt or maintain his survival. When the bible speaks of the man or woman being blessed who are fortunate enough to experience the joys of parenthood, it causes us to reflect on the condition of those who have been fortunate enough to have many arrows (children). It has been said, however, that this may be completely the opposite for those who are unable to have a full quiver.

When I think about this scripture and the personal experiences of my wife and I not being able to have any children, or the reverse of what is referenced in Psalms 127:5 (i.e., us having an empty quiver), an old television commercial comes to my mind, one of the top fifty commercials of all time. Launched in 1971 by a nonprofit organization called "Keep America Beautiful", it pictures a Native American man surrounded by an area that is so polluted, it causes tears to stream down his face (The True Story of the Crying Indian n.d.).

This is what I picture in my mind when I think of a man or woman wanting to have a child (as referred to in Psalms 127:5), but are unable to. I can see him, or her, in my mind, looking at their empty quiver with a tear or two streaming down their face. This scripture and that scene are what helped to inspire the idea and the title for this book.

As the tears stream down the eyes of the man who played the Native Indian disappointed over what he sees as the condition of his land, so is the sadness and the hurt found in the eyes and the hearts of many of those who have experienced the loss of a child or who are unable to bear children.

Chapter 2
THE QUESTION OF WHEN OR HOW MANY

Shirley and I were making plans for our future, planning to be married on June 6, 1981. We were very excited, as any young couple in love would be! One of the questions I remember asking her was, "How many kids do you think we'll have?" We would often laugh thinking there was just no telling how many children we'd end up with. There was a good reason I was curious about this question. I was the next to the youngest of six children on my side of the family, and Shirley was the youngest of twenty children by her mom on her side of the family. Therefore, we felt it was just natural to think of the possibilities of us having a large family. We thought we would possibly have at least three children, if not four. I also remember wondering just how soon it would be before we would have our first child. There was never the thought that we would not be able to bear children or even have any difficulties in attempting to have a child. At that time, little did my wife and I know that we would begin a journey which would bring us through many ups and downs and cause us both, as well as our family and friends, to shed many tears. We ultimately found ourselves asking the question, "Will we be able to have a child at all or is it just our purpose in life to mentor other children and not have our own?"

"As arrows are in the hand of a mighty man; so are children of the youth. Happy is the man that hath his quiver full of them: they shall not be ashamed, but they shall speak with the enemies in the gate."
(*Psalms 127:4-5, King James Version*)

After about a year and a half of being married, my wife raised the question again, "I wonder; when are we going to have a baby? I thought for sure we would have had one or two by now." We laughed and shrugged it off, thinking nothing of it at first. But then, after some time, we began to consider that we're not using any form of birth control or consciously doing anything to prevent conception so why is it, then, that we do not have a child?

From that point on, it seemed as though our main focus began to shift to that of having a child and wondering why we had not had one yet. For the first time in our marriage, we began to be concerned that there may be a problem with us conceiving. While we both had some initial concerns, we were still confident that if we gave it a little more time, we would soon be having our own beautiful bouncing bundle of joy in our home.

According to data from the U.S. Census Bureau and the Centers for Disease Control, who keep track of this sort of information, American women are an average age of 26 when they get married and 29 when they have their first child."

Shirley and I were both about twenty-five years old. We share the same birth month year and date. Although we were still young, many of our friends our age and some who had been married a lot less time than us, were beginning to start their families. At that time, even though we were still young, it seemed as if we had been married for a much longer period. We began to become deeply concerned about our ability to bear children.

In an article in the *US News and World Report*, it talks about the reaction to women who have decided to have a child and after taking a pregnancy test and finding the results are negative: "It can feel like a cruel game of hide and seek" (Miller, 2016).

While my wife was attempting to get pregnant, every month was an adventure. If her menstrual cycle went past thirty days, she would get excited. However, if on the thirty-first or thirty-second day she realized she was not pregnant, she would often fall into somewhat of a slump of despair. She would become very sad and disappointed. To the best of my ability, I would often try to encourage her to hang on in there.

This was like a never-ending cycle. She would get excited for a moment, feeling confident that she had gotten pregnant, only to find out a few days later she was not. It was as if Mother Nature was playing a cruel trick on her. The only problem was that Shirley and I were not laughing.

Many of the norms of today have changed and many women chose not to pursue motherhood until later on in life. This is still a changing trend and many would-be mothers find themselves challenged when it comes to their ability to bear a child. Due to advances in technology, many women who would not otherwise be able to bear a child, now have many more effective and better options that they can try to help them have a baby. The aid of modern science gives a greater sense of hope for the possibility of childbirth to those women who otherwise would not be able to have a child through the natural childbearing process.

One of the things I noticed in my generation, especially in the church, is that from the time you were married, the countdown would begin toward the day when you and your spouse would have your first child.

Another thing I have noticed is that many churches are against the use of contraceptives, encouraging young families to allow God to control how many children they have. After all, God knows how many children He wants you to birth. The problem with that is that when a young family has too many kids, more than they can financially handle, those same people will whisper behind their backs, "I wonder when they are going to stop having all those kids?"

Many churches have grown in size because of the idea that women should not take any contraceptives, and if they have more children than they are financially or emotionally able to handle, then this is just the will of God. There has been a stigma placed on men and woman who choose to delay childbearing, due primarily to the scripture admonishing Noah to reproduce and multiply. I could go on talking about this subject, women and men and the use of contraceptives in the church, but I will save that topic for another time.

Chapter 3
INFERTILITY/BARRENNESS

The bible shares with us many interesting stories regarding women who, for one reason or another, were barren. During biblical times their condition was looked upon as being cursed by God. John Byron, Professor at Ashland Theological Seminary writes, "Childlessness, in the Hebrew Bible is, presented as particularly a female problem. There are no biblical stories that center on an infertile man. The imagery of barrenness is never applied to a man" (2011).

Seven notable women in the bible were barren. These women were Sarai (the wife of Abraham), Rebekah (the wife of Isaac), Rachel (the wife of Jacob), the mother of Sampson, the wife of Manoah, Hannah (the wife of Elkanah and the mother of Samuel), Micah (the wife of David and daughter of King Saul), and Elizabeth (the wife of Zacharias, and mother of John the Baptist).

Karla Hawkins talks about how many cultures place a value on a woman based on her ability to bear children. She talks about how a woman's value would go up even more if she were to have a male child (2015).

Scripture also bears out the fact that women were looked at, or in many cases, perceived themselves to be, less of a woman if they were unable to bear children. (Note: In many cases, this may have just been their own personal perception). When we look at the story of Leah and Rachel in the Bible, we see two women competing for the love, acceptance, and the affection of their husband. As each woman would bear a child, the other felt that by giving her husband another child, he would love her more.

> *"And Leah conceived, and bare a son,*
> *and she called his name Reuben: for she said,*
> *Surely the Lord hath looked upon my affliction;*
> *now therefore my husband will love me."*
> *(Genesis 29:32, King James Version).*

I agree with Hawkins as she states, "Not everyone can have children though, so it has been a source of pain and suffering for many families through the years. Fortunately, a woman's value today is not based solely on her fertility, but rather on the many other gifts and talents she might possess." (Hawkins, 2015).

Chapter 4
WHAT IS THE PROBLEM? THE TEST!

Even though I had never said anything to my wife, the desire to be a father was always in the back of my mind. The thing that was most important to me, however, was to see my wife happy, regardless of whether or not we would be able to have a child of our own.

My wife, at this time, was not able to conceive a child. It seemed as though maybe we would never be able to have a child of our own. We were beginning to become frustrated at this point, not really knowing exactly what to do. We prayed and did our part, but nothing seemed to work. We were somewhat frustrated with the uncertainty of not knowing if we would be able to have a child, and a feeling of helplessness set in, not knowing what we could do beyond what we had already tried.

My wife came to me one day and said her doctor recommended that we see a fertility specialist. He suggested that we both have ourselves checked out for any underlying problems that either of us had that would prevent us from being able to birth a child. I was not too receptive to this suggestion. "Why, why would I want to have to subject myself to all of this? I am fine", I told myself. I do not need to be to taking any kind of tests. After all, I had the notion that a real man would not want to put himself through that. Therefore, I told my wife, "No way! I am not going through all that. If God wants us to have a child, it will just happen."

I then went on to try to encourage her by saying it would be just a little while and God would bless us with a child.

I asked myself, "Do I really believe what I am saying, or am I just saying it to ease my wife's concerns regarding having a child?" At this point, my personal faith in us becoming parents had begun to wane. I now questioned whether it was the will of God for us to have a child or was it God's will for us to be childless. Maybe God had some other plans for the Walton family. Maybe God wanted us to adopt. I was open to a number of options at this point. I just was not sure exactly what to think anymore.

I asked myself many times, after that conversation I had with my wife about us seeing a fertility specialist, was it just that I did not want to go because of my faith in God, or was it because somehow, in my mind, as a man, I just did not feel right about the idea of seeing a fertility specialist? I strongly believed in trusting God and thought maybe the reason I did not want to go see a specialist was because it felt as though I was not putting my trust in God.

The Church teaches us, that we should just trust in God for everything. Years ago, I can remember, and some churches practice it even today, that going to the doctor was a sin. They used a number of scriptures to support this thinking. One scripture is,

"Thus saith the LORD; Cursed be the man that trusteth in man, and maketh flesh his arm, and whose heart departeth from the LORD."
(*Jeremiah 17:5, King James Version*)

Another reason I had for not wanting to see a specialist was because I thought, "What if something is wrong with me?" Would I be able to handle the fact that there was a problem with me? How could I face myself if I were not able to father a biological child? Would that affect my male ego? Could I deal with that the rest of my life? I had a serious struggle with this. As I struggled, I decided that I did not want to take the test. On the other hand, I thought, "How would I ever know if I were alright or not?" Then I thought, if I did have a problem, maybe it was something simple that could easily be corrected.

After about a year of pondering the issue and Shirley not being too happy with my previous decision, I felt I owed it to her to do whatever we could do to eliminate all possible problems. I decided, it would be better to deal with the problem directly and accept whatever would be, but did it have to be now? I made up my mind that I would take the test but just was not quite sure when would be the best time to do it. Days went by, weeks went by, and even months. Whenever Shirley would question me about it, I would say, "Just give me a little more time."

Shirley was so determined for us to take the test, that she did a lot of research on the subject and had plenty of material to show me about it. When she tried to share the material with me, I would say thank you, act as if I was interested in it, take the material but never read it. The material stayed on my desk for a long while. It stayed on my desk for so long, I had actually forgotten about it, but Shirley had not. This thing was quite serious with her.

Hoping that somehow, things would blow over and she would give up on the idea, I never spoke on the subject again. Shirley came to me later and asked if I had read the material yet. My answer to her was no. I could feel and see the frustration that was building up over it. At this point, I came to the resolve that I could not put it off any longer. In Shirley's mind, my putting off the test was as if I was not concerned about her feelings, which was not the case.

I finally found myself becoming more curious as to what the outcome would be, so I told Shirley to schedule the test. I will never forget the expression on her face when I told her. It was as if I were asking her to marry me all over again. My refusal to take the test made her feel as though I had fallen out of love with her and was not willing to validate any of her feelings. Now by agreeing to take the test, I had fallen back in love with her again. A weight had seemingly fallen off her shoulders. After watching her expression, I knew at that point, I had made the right decision.

Shirley made the appointment and told me to make sure I marked the date on my calendar. She advised me not to make any other plans for that date. Up until the date of the appointment, she would often remind me about it. "Two more weeks, five more days, tomorrow is the big day", she would say.

As I prepared to take the test, I began to read the literature she had provided me. It contained a great deal of valuable information. Recently I read, in a survey of married women, the CDC found that 1.5 million women in the US (6%) are infertile (Source: National Survey of Family Growth, Centers for Disease Control and Prevention [CDC] 2006-2010). Twenty-five percent of infertile couples have more than one factor that contributes to their infertility. I realized that we were not alone! Looking back, I would now encourage any couple having problems conceiving a child to exhaust all of their options and not give up.

The day finally came when we were scheduled to take the test. The day was somewhat stressful for me, as I was very anxious about the possible outcomes. I wonder what the office would look. Would there be bells and whistles, and what would the people working there be like?

I was very surprised at what I saw. I can remember the doctor talking quite calmly to Shirley and me and being very understanding of our feelings as he shared with us the many possible outcomes of the test. To me, the whole situation was as if I was having a dream. Asking myself, "Was all this real?" Why weren't we like normal couples and not having to go through all of this? I remember thinking that most couples have children and give it very little thought. I had a million questions running through my mind, but at the same time, I had to listen to what the doctor was telling us. I tried desperately to take it all in. As I watched Shirley's expressions, I would give her a reassuring smile that everything was going to be all right.

As I prepared to take the test, and the nurse led me to a private room, I asked myself, "What in the world am I doing here?" The sooner I could get out of the office and go about my business, the better off I would be. I could not leave the room until I had left a specimen for the doctor to examine. After I took the test, I thought I would leave the doctor's office with the results, but that would not be the case. We were told we would have to do a number of tests and then the doctor would be getting back with us.

As I waited for the results, days went by, weeks went by, and even a few months went by before we were able to get the results back. I thought, now I know how Shirley must have felt when I had her to wait while I was deciding when and if I was going to have the tests done. Now the tables were turned. It was now me waiting with feelings of anxiety of what we would be hearing from the doctor. Finally, we received that call that the test was completed and they wanted us to come into the office to explain the results. The call was on a Monday and the appointment was for Friday. I questioned if we could get in before Friday (the suspense was killing me), but they said that was the first available time we could be seen.

When we got to our appointment, the doctor spoke with us in many technical terms but all I really wanted to hear was, "Mr. Walton, you checked out ok." Using more medical terminology that I had no idea of what he was saying, he finally says in a calm manner, "Mr. Walton, we don't see any abnormalities with your tests or any areas to be concerned about, you checked out fine." I wanted to shout, "Y-E-S, Y-E-S, Y-E-S! I'm alright!" I felt at that moment that my manhood could stay intact.

After the immediate pleasure of knowing I was all right, I began to realize that I had been selfish in my thinking, and now turned my attention to how Shirley was feeling. Was the problem with her? I questioned in my mind, "Where do we go from here?" However, I knew one thing for sure; we would be in this together. As I looked into Shirley's eyes, I could see a sadness that while I was excited for my results, for her the hope that the problem was not with her was equally as great as mine was for the problem not being with me.

Chapter 5
SHE WANTS TO HAVE MY BABY BUT SHE'S NOT MY WIFE

It is funny how when you have plenty of something, that you often take it for granted and do not even think about it. However, the minute you think, you want it or feel deprived of it, it seems to consume the majority of your time. I just took it for granted that my wife and I would not have any problems having a child. Now that I found out that I checked out ok and there was no problem with me physically, I had a certain confidence in myself once I realized the problem was not with me. However, in the back of my mind, I struggled with the idea that now I really wanted to have a biological child. I wondered what it would be like; a child that had my genes. A child that had eyes that looked like mine, that I could say he or she was a part of me.

    I worked for the phone company during this time; very young, very attractive, and very intelligent women surrounded me. I tried to carry myself as a young Christian man with integrity. I would always wear my wedding ring to let them know I was married and unavailable. It was common knowledge that my wife and I had a good relationship, but it was also common knowledge that we were unable to have children. Being one of only three men in an office with mostly women, I often had to deal with friendly flirtation. For the most part, it was an occasional sweet talk or maybe someone saying, "I sure wish you weren't married, why it is that all the good men are taken?"

I would even have a few to tell me "You're married and you're a Christian, but you're still human and if you get tired of your wife, just call me".

There was this one woman named LaToya, (fictitious name) who would make it a point to try to get my attention every day. The more I tried to ignore her, the more she tried to get my attention. One day, LaToya was wearing an outfit that was somewhat revealing and she asked me, "Now what could you do with all this?" As usual, I ignored her. I just shook my head and refused to respond.

During this time, the thought of being a father was constantly on my mind. Whenever I would see a couple with a child, I would think to myself just how nice it would be to have a son or a daughter.

LaToya approached me another day as I was getting on the elevator. She looked at me and said in a sultry voice, "If your wife can't give you a baby, I can give you one." I must admit, her words took me by surprise. For a second I was speechless and when I got myself together, I said, "No thanks!" She just smiled and said, "I believe we could make some good babies. Just let me know if you change your mind." The elevator doors opened and we both got off and went our separate ways. Nothing more was said again regarding that conversation. From that point on, I made it my business to go out of my way to avoid LaToya.

"No one begins a marriage expecting to cheat on their spouse. According to the Journal of Couples and Relationship Therapy, approximately 50 percent of

married women and 60 percent of married men will have an extramarital affair at some time in their marriage."
(Shugerman, n.d.)

Something happened to me that day when LaToya spoke with me. I began to feel as Abraham did when he wanted to have a son. Sarah was beyond the age of childbearing and, for all practical purposes, would not be able to give him a child. Shirley was not beyond childbearing age, as we were both quite young at the time, in our twenties. However, we both felt like we were getting older and uncertain if she would be able to bear us a child. We talked about adopting a child, which I was fine with, but I still wanted a biological child of my own.

Shirley would often speak of her desire to bear children. I would assure her that someday we would have a son or a daughter together, but in the back of my mind, I would wonder if this was just me dreaming. Yet I tried to keep the faith for the both of us. She would at times become depressed over not being able to have a child, not to the point that she was not functioning, but I could tell it in her actions. I could tell it in her expression whenever we were around a couple who just had a new baby. There was something different. She did not have that same glowing smile that I was used to seeing.

I purposed in my heart that if Shirley and I could not have a baby together, then we would adopt. I made a commitment to my wife when we got married that we would be together for better or worse. This was not the worse, but it was a tremendous challenge to our faith as well as to my fidelity to our marriage. I decided that I would do the right thing and hang on in there with Shirley. I'd either trust in the Lord for her to become pregnant or accept the fact that having children may not be the will of God for our lives.

"Now Sarai Abram's wife bare him no children: and she had a handmaid, an Egyptian, whose name was Hagar. And Saria said unto Abram, Behold now, the Lord hath restrained me from bearing: I pray thee, go in unto my maid, it may be that I may obtain children by her. And Abram hearkened to the voice of Sarai."
(Genesis 16:1-2, King James Version)

Chapter 6
I'M PREGNANT

After a few years of wanting to have a baby, which seemed like a lifetime, Shirley finally shared with me the good news that we were both waiting to hear. She was pregnant! We were both very excited at the idea of becoming new parents.

Although Shirley was pregnant, and because there was no reason for concern at this point, she continued to work. We pretty much went about our normal schedule, with the exception that every week (if not every day) Shirley would buy something for the new baby. She would drag me along with her to the different baby stores and, because I hated shopping, I would try to act as if I was just as excited as she was. Seeing Shirley happy with baby shopping put a smile on my face as well. I was thrilled at the fact we were finally going to have a child.

Even though we were both excited, the closer we got to her having the baby, the stress of becoming a parent was starting to get to me. I wondered if I could handle the waking up at night, the feeding the baby, the changing the diapers etc. I also was concerned about the financial obligations. Shirley and I had been married for about seven years and we had (at least I had) become comfortable traveling all over the country at our leisure and just having fun. Even though we waited and prayed for this moment, I realized it was not coming without a certain amount of sacrifice. On one hand, I wanted to be selfish and continue the freedom that we had grown accustomed to, but on the other hand, we both were extremely delighted at the thought of having a newborn baby in our home.

Chapter 7
THE EARLY LABOR

It was Thursday, May 12, 1988. It started out as a very good day. I was up early and had an early breakfast, which was typical. I usually would not leave out the door for work unless I had a good breakfast. I went to work and was looking forward to a good evening as we were having a youth service for our state young people. I was the Treasurer and knew it would be a busy evening for me, but I really did not mind the work at all. I enjoyed my position working with the young people, and strove to do the best I could in that position. While I was at work, I called back home to check on my wife to see how she was feeling. This was a daily habit I had started, and especially now that she was expecting. She said she felt a little tired, but other than that, she was feeling fine.

Later that evening when I got home from work, I again asked my wife how she was feeling, she said, "Ok", but I don't think I feel like going out to church tonight. You go ahead and enjoy yourself." I went to the service and had a great time. After the service was over, a group of young people and I all went out to eat. I called my wife prior to my going and asked if she wanted me to bring her anything. She said no and so we all went out and had a fun time.

When I got home, it was about 10:45 pm. I was tired from working, going to church and going out to eat after church. As soon as my head hit the pillow, I was out like a light. About twenty minutes into my sleep, I could hear my wife moving around and I could tell something was not right. She advised me she was bleeding and did not feel good. Immediately I jumped up, called the doctor who told us to go immediately to the emergency room. As I was driving her to the hospital, I believe I ran every light between home and the hospital. All I was concerned about at that time was getting her to the hospital, getting her checked out, and making sure she and the baby were both going to be all right.

When the doctor saw her, he set us both down and said it did not look good. The doctor explained to us that Shirley was going into pre-mature labor, and that there was a strong possibility that we would be losing the baby. He went on to say that, the next twenty-four hours would be the most crucial period, but if the baby made it through the night there would be a greater chance of the baby's survival.

Shirley was in shock as well as myself. We never expected anything like this to happen. I tried my best to encourage her. I knew how bad she wanted this child. I knew what it meant to her to be able to hold a little one of her own in her arms however, there was nothing that I could do except be there to support her, and pray.

In the story of Hezekiah in the bible, expecting to die.

"In those days was Hezekiah sick unto death. And Isaiah the prophet the son of Amoz came unto him, and said, Thus saith the Lord, Set thine house in order: for thou shalt die, and not live. Then Hezekiah turned his face toward the wall, and prayed unto the Lord."
(Isaiah 38:1-2, King James Version)

I turned my face to the wall and began to talk to God. I began to pray and ask God to just let the child make it through the delivery. I was not asking for myself, but for Shirley. For her to have the experience of delivering a child was my request to God. If the Lord did not choose to extend the child's life, then my prayer was for God to just help him make it through the night.

Now I am not superstitious or anything like that, but the next day was Friday the thirteenth. I thought it would be a good day for me if the child could only make it through the night. All I could do was pray and hope for the best. I continually turned my face to the wall and talked to God as Hezekiah did.

In 2015, about one out of ten babies was born too early in the United States...
Premature (also known as preterm) birth is when a baby is born too early, before 37 weeks of pregnancy. The earlier a baby is born, the higher the risk of death or serious disability. In 2013, about one-third (36%) of infant deaths were due to preterm-related causes. Babies who survive can have breathing issues, intestinal (digestive) problems, and bleeding in their brains. Long-term problems may include developmental delay (not meeting the developmental milestones for his or her age) and lower performance in school (Center for Disease Control, 2015).

We were blessed when our son was born. Against all odds, he made it through the first 24 hours. The doctor told us not to be overly optimistic because our child was going to have a rough road ahead of him, and many challenges to overcome. We were just excited that he had made it this far. I decided that we would enjoy whatever time the Lord allowed us to have with our son.

As we watched our son make it through the first week, then the second, then a month, we began to become a little more optimistic that his chances of survival were good. At first, I felt there was very little hope of him surviving, even though Shirley felt as though he was going to be all right. I always hoped for the best but was not overly optimistic, and was preparing for the worst. I would tell Shirley, "Do not get your hopes up too high in case things do not go well." I was trying to prepare her in case things got worse. I did not want her to be devastated. To some this would appear as if I did not have much faith. My faith was very strong, but at the same time I thought, *God let your will be done.*

For the next few days, weeks, and months, we would spend countless hours in the neo-natal intensive care unit just watching our son, talking with him and encouraging him to hold on. It was amazing to watch him grow. He was less than two pounds at birth and was now slowly but surely gaining weight as the doctors and nurses would feed him the nutrients he needed to grow.

I would go to see him every day, before I went to work, around 5:30 a.m. or 6:30 a.m., stay for about an hour or hour and a half, and then go to work. I would go right back to the hospital after I got off from work for about another hour or two.

His face would simply light up as Shirley or I would talk with him. The doctor told us this was therapeutic for him. Even though going to the hospital twice a day was quite draining on the both of us, we did not mind it at all. That was our son and he was fighting for his very life.

As I looked around at all the other babies struggling to live, I believed that because we were Christians and many there were not, our son would have a better chance of surviving and coming home. I looked around at some of the other babies seeing how they were in a much worse condition than our son was. Surely because we try to live right and do the right thing, surely, because we prayed daily, surely, because we went to church on a regular basis, we did not have a thing to worry about. God was testing our faith but after he got finish testing us, we would come out of this with a testimony. We would come out with a testimony, but not the one we expected.

As the days went by, some of the other babies transferred out to the nursery and were able to go home. However, some of the babies we would see one day and they would not have made it through to the next day.

My faith increased to the point to where, for the first time during this whole ordeal, I just knew he was going to be all right. After all, I was a child of God and this was only a test of my faith. If I could just believe, hold on to my faith, I knew things would get better.

After about three months, things were looking up and the doctor told us on Tuesday that he would be able to come home on the following Monday. For the first time since his birth, I believed that he was going to be all right, that my little son would be coming home. I was now really excited and anticipating him coming home with Shirley and me.

      I would go every day to visit my son. This was my daily routine. I would get excited to see the amount of improvement he would be making on a daily basis. He was getting stronger and stronger every day. It would always be a joy to see how he would respond to me when I would come to see him. The nurses and doctors all were optimistic, and so were Shirley and I, that our son would be coming home any day now. As I left the hospital, I looked at him with his small little eyes and told him that I would see him in the morning. Shirley was not with me. I had gone to the hospital straight from work. Even though I hated to leave him, I knew I was tired and would be right back to see him, first thing in the morning.

Chapter 8
THE PHONE CALL

I had only been home from the hospital for about an hour. Just long enough to clean up and prepare to get something to eat. I had not had anything to eat. I guess with everything that was going on at the time, I really did not have much of an appetite. It was on a Wednesday, about 8:00 pm as I had just begun to get relaxed when we got a phone call from the hospital. I knew it was from the hospital because we could hear the machines beeping in the background. This was not strange, because we were used to the sounds of the machines in the neo-natal ICU by now, but something was different this time. I could hear it in the nurse's voice. She tried to sound calm but I could hear the sadness in her voice. This was the call that we had so sorely dreaded receiving when our son was first born. We thought we had gotten past all this and that next call we would be receiving from the hospital would be to hear them say, "You can come and pick up your son to take him home with you," but this call was not about that. Our son had taken a turn for the worse, according to the hospital staff. The nurse told us on the phone that one of the other nurses had tried to pull a breathing tube from our son. He stopped breathing, and we needed to get to the hospital right away.

We were devastated. This was not expected. I just left the hospital about an hour before and he was looking fine. I was excited about him being able to come home within the next few days. How could this have happened within just a short time? It was as if I was having a bad nightmare. It felt like I had been hit by a ton of bricks.

When we got to the hospital, the story changed. The nurse said they were getting ready to feed him and he just stopped breathing. Shirley and I were in disbelief. I had just gotten to the place for the first time where I felt comfortable enough to let my guard down. I had just begun to believe he would be all right, and now this happens. Shirley and I did not know what to do but cry. We were both simply numb. It all just seemed to be so surreal, as if we were in a very bad dream. I wanted someone to pinch me and tell me this was not happening to us, but that never happened. Our son was dying, and there was nothing, we, the nurses, the doctors, or anyone else could do about it.

I remember thinking as I was sad, hurting, and in pain that all the prayers that went up did not prevent his death. It was hard for me to look at my son. I was used to him responding when I came near him, but this time everything was different. He was not responding. My heart was so heavy I could barely handle it. I was angry that I was not able to protect Shirley from the pain of this loss, no matter how bad I wanted to. I could not even protect myself. I was in a deep state of shock. I just did not know what to do. All I could do was to hold Shirley and fight back the tears.

The doctor asked us if we wanted to call our pastor. We thought that would be a good idea. We called our pastor. He and his wife came to the hospital to support us. It was such a sad scene that the pastor and his wife began to cry along with us. The nurses and even the doctor were crying.

The staff just looked at us as if they did not know what to say or do. It was a very sad and emotional moment for all of us. No one could think of the right words to say at a time like this. I remember the doctor just looking at us, and then giving Shirley a hug and rubbing my shoulders, as to say I feel your pain, but I do not know what I can say to help. She knew there were no amount of words she could say at that time that would ease our pain. Only God and time would give us the comfort that we needed. At that moment, it felt as if even that would be hard. Being a Christian, I had faith in God. I knew that God could give a person comfort in the time of sorrow. I knew many comforting scriptures, but for some reason, I could not think of any scriptures or did not want to think of them. I was sad and hurting. I felt that I would never get over the pain I was feeling. Even today, many years later, as I relive the events of that terrible, horrible night, I can still fill much of the pain that I felt on that night.

As I looked at how the staff was reacting, I thought to myself, this is not the first time they had lost a child in this neo-ICU unit. The staff said this was not the first time, but they were all rooting for our son. He was a special child. He possessed such a unique spirit even as an infant. The nurses and doctors would often tell us that there was just something different about him. I knew and felt in my heart there was something different about him. This feeling and belief made his death that much harder for me to accept. There was something different about him that touched the hearts of all those who cared for him. Yes, he was special, not because he was our son, but also because, even in his death, I had hope in the fact that I believed God had a reason for his short life. There had to be a purpose in all of this. Now he was gone. I tried to fight back the tears, but I just could not. My heart was so heavy. I tried to keep it together enough to support Shirley but she, instead, began to hold and encourage me almost more than I did her.

Chapter 9
THE DEATH/ FUNERAL/RETURNING BABY FURNITURE

Now as a young couple, having just lost our son, we now faced with the challenge of planning for his funeral. How do you begin such a task? I never in a thousand years would have imagined my wife and I being in this position, a young couple making funeral arrangements for our son. The staff said we could spend as much time as we wanted before they took him away. They said we could go home and call them back when we decided how we were going to handle the arrangements.

"Holding a funeral or a special memorial service for your baby is a beautiful, personal way of saying goodbye. It allows you the opportunity to honor your baby's life in a way that is unique and significant to you" (Bears of Hope, 2016).

After talking with family and friends as well as members of the clergy, we decided to have a small funeral at the funeral chapel. Through talking with others, we were encouraged to have a service.

We were convinced, having the service would help with the grieving process. I realized that Shirley and I were not the only ones who were grieving over our loss, that our family and friends who cared about us were also touched by our son's brief life.

The Friday afternoon of the funeral, we only expected a few close family members and friends to show up, but to our amazement, the funeral home was packed.

There were friends and family, as well as staff from the hospital, and a number of my co-workers who had come to share their support for us during this time of our loss.

The service was a blessing to my wife and me as well as to all those who came to give us comfort and support. I can still remember some of the clergy who took time out of their busy schedules to lend their support for us during our loss: Bishop Gary Burt, Bishop Joseph Farris, Bishop Benjamin T Moore Sr., and Bishop Michael Shelby.

These pastors all delivered encouraging words that helped us not only to get through the service, but words that were able to inspire and lift our spirits as we had to deal with the immediate loss and the events following the loss of our son.

After the funeral service for our son, we were glad that we chose to have a home going service for him. It presented us with a certain amount of closure, after he had experienced such a hard fought battle for the short time he was in this cruel, cold and sometimes uncaring world.

The support and love of those who came allowed the healing process to begin. It helped us prepare for the next chapter in our lives that we at times found to be overwhelming. At times, we found ourselves struggling through in order to find some relief from our hurt and pain. The support of so many family and friends showed us that when you do not think people are concerned about you, there are people who support and are praying for you, even if they never say a word to you. When some of our loved ones did not know what to say to Shirley and me, they were able to talk to God about it.

One of the most difficult and heart wrenching things for Shirley and I to do was to take the baby furniture back to the store. We purchased so much furniture and had no one to give it to, so we decided to take it all back. We had not used any of it. When we got to the store, they were excited to see us. We had established a relationship with the sales people. The first thing they said was, "How is your new baby?" We had to tell them that he had passed. I could look into their faces and see how uncomfortable they felt at that moment. It was as if they wanted to get us out of there as soon as possible, not because they were upset with us, but because they realized how awkward it was for all of us. They looked sad and at a loss for words. They said they understood, and it would not be a problem for us to return the merchandise. They gladly accepted the returned items. This took a lot of pressure off of us. It was hard for us to have the baby furniture in our home. It was a reminder of all we had gone through. During this time, even simple little things became quite emotional for the both of us. We were very appreciative of the kindness and understanding expressed by the clerks, even more than they realized.

Chapter 10
WILL LOVE KEEP US TOGETHER?

Licensed Marriage & Family Therapist Jean Galica, M.A., discusses what many believe to be the effects on the family of those who have suffered the loss of a child in their marriage. In trying to dispel some myths, she writes, "The actual facts bear out that the death of a child usually acts, instead, to polarize the existing factors found in the marriage; hence, some marriage gets worse, some get better, some just maintain, and some actually do end in divorce" (Galica, n.d.).

Many have also told me, including my psychology professor, that my wife and I were the only couple they knew whose marriage survived the loss of a child. The loss of our son definitely put our marriage to the test. There were so many different emotions coming from the both of us. Sometimes we wanted to talk. Then there were times when either Shirley or I would just shut ourselves off from the other. One thing that was good was that we never played the blame game. Many people, when they are hurt and do not know who to blame, start finding a reason to blame the other person. The reason does not have to be a valid one. This is what you would call displaced aggression. You are upset with someone else, in this case God, and you take it out on the closest person to you, your spouse.

I knew of a couple who lost their son. They were an older couple in their late forties. The husband wanted to have another son to carry on his name. Because the wife was unable to bear him a child, he divorced her and married a much younger woman. His desire to have a son was more important to him than that of keeping his marriage together. His new wife was much younger and able to bear him children but the age difference caused him a number of other challenges.

During the days following the death of our son and his funeral, my wife and I really did not know what to say. Sometimes we would talk to each other, sharing our feelings, and sometimes we would just be quiet. There were times when we would hold and embrace each other and other times when we were both hurt, angry, moody, and just wanting to be left alone.

We found ourselves having to face many challenges. We often felt as though we were fighting an uphill battle that showed no end in sight. Even though there was a lot of emotional strain on the both of us, we never talked of leaving each other. We did have times when we found ourselves overwhelmed by everything and there was a great deal of tension between the two of us initially, but we had decided at the onset that we would work things out no matter how difficult they became.

One of the many challenges we had to face was the enormous medical bills that we had to pay. Our son's hospital bill had reached well over a million dollars. With everything else we had to deal with, this was just one more concern. Even after our son's death, the insurance company billed us for services that he had not received.

We realize that everything we had to encounter would be a true test of our love for each other, as well as our love for God. It is one thing to say that "I'm going through no matter what the test" but it is entirely different when you find yourself actually going through the biggest test of your life up to that point. It is good to say, "I'll trust in God no matter what," but when you are in the Lion's den and the lions are licking their lips, what are you going to do then? This was a test like no other, one that neither of us had ever experienced. This would either make or break our faith in God.

"Charity suffereth long, and is kind; charity envieth not; charity vaunteth not itself, is not puffed up, Doth not behave itself unseemly, seeketh not her own, is not easily provoked, thinketh no evil; Rejoiceth not in iniquity, but rejoiceth in the truth; Beareth all things, believeth all things, hopeth all things, endureth all things, Charity never faileth:"
(*1 Corinthians 13:4-8, King James Version*)

During our most difficult times, Shirley and I would often quote this scripture and remind ourselves that our love for each other would endure and allow us to overcome any and everything we had to face if we would just allow the spirit of God to lead us.

According to the U.S. National Center for Health Statistics, approximately 50,000 U.S. children die annually. They go on to say, "The death of a child is one of the most painful events that an adult can experience and is linked to complicated/traumatic grief reactions. The loss of a child can cause a number of emotional reactions from the parents and other family members such as severe anxiety, depression, and even guilt." (Rogers et al, 2016, p 203)

"In light of the significance of child death as a traumatic experience for parents, research on parental bereavement is more limited than might be expected." (Rogers C, 2016, p 203)

"Parents might also experience guilt about having been unable to protect the child" (Gilbert as cited in Rogers C, 2016, p 203).

In an article written by Judith Rollins Bohannon, she talks about how husbands and wives experience grief in different ways. She writes, "Grief Experience Inventory at three times over a one-year period." According to the study, significant differences were found between grief levels of spouses' responses and/or differences over time in 10 of 12 variables: denial, despair, and guilt, loss of control, rumination, depersonalization, somatization, death anxiety, vigor, and physical strength (Bohannon 1990-1991).

Chapter 11
THE QUESTION TO GOD, "WHY?"

I felt I was strong in my faith prior to this time. I would share my faith with anyone who was willing to listen. I spoke with many individuals who questioned their faith in God and I would tell them that what they were going through was just a test of their faith. I would tell them, "You can make it! Just keep the faith!"

Somehow, when Shirley and I were going through our test, I found myself questioning my faith in God, and everything I knew regarding God, up to this point. I kept asking myself, "If you love me, God, and I have done all I can do to live a Godly life, then why God, did you let this happen to us?"

I was angry, mad, hurt, disappointed, and frustrated. I knew Satan was trying his best to get me to the place where I would begin to consider giving up on my faith in the church as well as in God.

I began to ask God, "Why me, why my family, why my little son?" I even asked God why couldn't he have taken me and let my son live. So many things ran through my mind as I began to relive over, and, over, and over again the events of the previous seven to eight months.

"The thief cometh not, but for to steal, and to kill, and to destroy: I am come that they might have life, and that they might have it more abundantly."
(*John 10:10, King James Version*)

Seeing and knowing my faith was on trial, and that it was Satan, attempting to steal everything deposited in me, that was Godly. Satan was a thief, but I was determined I was not going to let him rob me of my faith in God, even though I knew my faith was being severely tested. I continued to seek the presence of God.

*"I sought the LORD, and he heard me,
and delivered me from all my fears."*
(*Psalms 34:4, King James Version*)

I was struggling with all we were going through, but I felt that if I would keep seeking the presence of God, He would eventually hear and deliver me.

Chapter 12
THE ANGER AND THE LOSS OF DESIRE TO PRAY

I was angry for a number of reasons. Primarily because of the loss of my son, but secondly because of the responses from many of the Christians who showed very little, if any, concern for our situation. I thought the church would embrace us, only to find out that many of those who I thought were our friends did not even reach out to us to show any sympathy or concern.

I found myself dealing with all kinds of emotions. I did not know exactly how to feel. How should I have felt? Should I just go on with my life as before or should I be angry with God? I did not know what to do with myself.

I tried to pray and I could not find the right words to say. I rehearsed in my mind, the scripture; **"Give thanks in every circumstance, for this is God's will for you in Christ Jesus."** (*1 Thessalonians 5:18, Berean Study Bible*). How could I and why would I want to give God thanks for taking my son? I asked myself, "How could I ever thank God for such a terrible loss? Is this really God's plan for Shirley and me?" If it was, we sure did not ask for it, and for sure was not happy about it.

After supporting my wife, I found myself at a point where I was mad and I felt I had the right to be mad. If anyone had a right to be angry, it was I. I had gone through something that I would not have wished on my worst enemy. I guess I was having a pity party. I knew that was what I was doing but I did not even care. After all, no one could possibly know or understand what I was going through, right? During this time, it was not about Shirley's hurt. I was being selfish. I was more concerned about my own feelings at that moment.

Whenever I would attempt to pray, all I could do was to focus on the pain I was feeling. I asked God to remove the pain from both Shirley and me. Whenever I would try to pray, my mind would just go blank. I knew I was not the only person who had endured hurt, who had suffered the loss of a child, but in all that we had gone through, I found it so hard to pray for myself, and even harder to pray for anyone else.

One thing that helped me in the process, that helped me in not giving up on prayer, regardless of how hard it seemed for me to pray, was a book by Donald E. Demaray entitled, *How Are You Praying*. He tells of the story of Mary and Martha, and how after Lazarus their brother had died, they were upset with Jesus. They knew Jesus had the power to heal their brother. If only he had intervened on their behalf, their brother would still be alive. I felt the same way. If God had only heard my prayer, or if he did hear my prayer, then why would he not do something about it? Why did God not grant me my partition?

Demaray asserts, "First, we cannot 'throw in the sponge.' We cannot say we suspected all along that prayer was a myth and that at last we have come to our mature senses. To give up faith in God is not the answer" (Demaray 1985, p 131).

While I was going through all of this, I found for the first time in my walk with Christ, it was even hard to go to church. I wanted to go to church, but I just did not want to answer questions about our son. How do you respond to a person when you are hurting and they ask, "How are you doing?" "Should I tell them I'm fine, when I know I'm really not? On the other hand, should I tell them the truth? A true answer would have been, "I feel awful; I feel like a big weight is on me just holding me down. I am angry and really do not feel like talking about it with you or anyone else. I'd rather be left alone right now." Now, I am sure that is not what they would want to hear. I realized, however, that some of the people who asked how I was doing really were not concerned or cared to hear how I felt at all. I remember a person asking me how I was doing. Rather than saying I was having a bad day, I said "Not well." Their response was, "That's good." They were not even listening to what I had to say.

I knew I had to pray my way through this, regardless of how I was feeling.

"And he spake a parable unto them to this end, that men ought always to pray, and not to faint;"
(Luke 18:1, King James Version)

Even though it was hard for me to pray, I decided to say a few short prayers daily.

I always knew the importance of prayer, and now, for the first time in my life, I found myself tested by a lack of desire to pray. I knew the scriptures told us that men should always pray, but I was not feeling a desire to pray. Instead, I felt that my praying was in vain and wondered if God was even listening to me.

There were those individuals who just blatantly asked, "What do you think is wrong? What have you or Shirley done to bring this upon you?" I now know in the midst of all I was going through, God had his hand on me or I would have expressed to these individuals just how I felt. At this space in time, I am not sure just how spiritual my response would have been. Thank God for having his hand over my life even when I did not realize it.

"Though he slay me, yet will I trust in him: but I will maintain mine own ways before him."
(Job 13:15, King James Version)

For about a year, I found my faith severely tested. Every time I would trust in God for something, it seemed as though whenever I attempted to put my trust in God, I would have the rug pulled out from under me. I wanted desperately to trust in God. What do you do when you decided to trust in God and it seemed as though no matter how big or small the matter was, in those moments when I would say to myself or anyone else that I believe God, the very thing I believed in Him for would just get worse.

I actually had gotten to the point that I was afraid to trust in God for anything. I wanted to, I really tried to, but I was just too afraid. I pray that no one else finds himself or herself in this position. The enemy thought he had me right where he wanted me.

Time after time, I attempted to believe God for something, and I would tell myself, "I know God's not going to let me down this time." Once again, just as soon as I felt as if I could trust in God, I would again be disappointed at the outcome. As this went on a number of times, I began to tell myself, "If I'm not going to have faith in God to deliver me or if I'm not going to trust in him then what will I do?" I thought about the scripture in the bible where Jesus proclaimed:

"Then Jesus said unto them, Verily, verily, I say unto you, Except ye eat the flesh of the Son of man, and drink his blood, ye have no life in you."
(John 6:53, King James Version)

After much soul searching, pain, and at times, disbelief, I finally came to the realization that there are moments in our lives when God places us on paths where we have no idea where or why He chooses to places us there. Nevertheless, we must ultimately make a decision, and the decision we make will determine our destiny in God. The question I often asked myself is, "what do you do when the place where God takes you is uncomfortable and you have no control. Do you give up? Do you throw in the towel? Do you take it out on others? Many times, I found myself in a position where my whole life seems to be out of control. I just wanted to give up and lean to my fleshly carnal nature.

I eventually got to the point where I had to say as the Apostle Peter said, "And Simon answering said unto him, Master we have toiled all the night, and have taken nothing: nevertheless, at thy world I will let down the net." As I learned how to turn things over to God, a peace began to come over me. Through all that I have been through, I thank God for bringing me through.

"There is a way that seemeth right unto a man, but the end thereof are the ways of death."
(Proverbs 16:25, King James Version)

When Jesus spoke to his disciples about the eating of his flesh and drinking of his blood, they found this to be too hard for them to comprehend. Not having the full understanding (Spiritual revelation) and not willing to trust completely in Jesus, the bible says many of them decided to just walk away from Jesus and his teachings.

This was my state of mind, I was not in a good place, but the spirit convicted me, and I could feel and understand in my spirit the response that Peter made when Jesus asked the twelve if they were ready to leave also?

"Then Simon Peter answered him, Lord, to whom shall we go? thou hast the words of eternal life.
And we believe and are sure that thou art that Christ, the Son of the living God."
(John 6:68-69, King James Version)

I was not sure what to do, but I knew I could not give up on God. I had to trust in Him, I had to hold on to see what His ultimate divine plan was for Shirley and me.

"O lord, thou hast searched me, and known me. Thou knowest my downsitting and mine uprising, thou understandest my thought afar off. Thou compassest my path and my lying down, and art acquainted with all my ways. For there is not a word in my tongue, but, lo, O LORD, thou knowest it altogether. Thou hast beset me behind and before, and laid thine hand upon me. Such knowledge is too wonderful for me; it is high, I cannot attain unto it. Whither shall I go from thy spirit? or whither shall I flee from thy presence? If I ascend up into heaven, thou art there: if I make my bed in hell, behold, thou art there. If I take the wings of the morning, and dwell in the uttermost parts of the sea; even there shall thy hand lead me, and thy right hand shall hold me."
(Psalms 139:1-10, King James Version)

"Yet I have left me seven thousand in Israel, all the knees which have not bowed unto Baal, and every mouth which hath not kissed him."
(1 Kings 19:18, King James Version)

I chose to do as Job did. I made up in my mind that whatever God allowed Shirley and me to go through that His grace would be more than enough to carry us through. I thought about those in the bible who sacrificed their very lives and here I am acting like Elijah when he proclaimed as if he was the only one living for God or the only one that was having troubles. God's response to him was:

"Yet I have left me seven thousand in Israel, all the knees which have not bowed unto Baal, and every mouth which hath not kissed him."
(1 Kings 19:18, King James Version)

Whenever you think, you are alone and no one else has gone through what you have gone through or have suffered the same kind of loss, remember you are not alone. Others have often had to endure much worse than you and I, and have been able to overcome it and proclaim God's victory over their situation.

"And he spake a parable unto them to this end, that men ought always to pray, and not to faint;"
(Luke 18:1, King James Version)

Why is it Necessary to Pray?

Knowing how important it was for me to pray, I made it a habit of having my personal daily prayer and devotion long before this happened with our son. When this day came and I did not feel to pray, I believe because I had committed myself to prayer in the past, I was more aware that me not praying was not my normal state and I felt extremely uncomfortable with not praying.

It is when a man or woman of God is at his or her lowest point that the need for prayer and bible reading is even more essential in their lives. The scriptures in Matthew 4:11 illustrate this: when after Jesus had fasted forty days and forty nights, being led up into the wilderness to be tempted (tested) of the devil. We are aware that Satan comes to destroy a person at their weakest point. My wife and I were very vulnerable at this point to the attacks of the enemy. We had just experienced the loss of our son and our emotions were all over the place. We are thankful to God we were covered by the prayers of our family and friends even when we did not want to pray. This is a point in the life of a Christian when the importance of having intercessory pray warriors is most important - those who will go to the throne of God on someone's behalf. I'm sure there were many praying for us, but because of the state we were in, we could not see them. But I now know they were out there and constantly holding us up before God.

Chapter 13
THE DESIRE TO BE LEFT ALONE

As my wife and I attempted to process all that was happening to us, at times, we had a number of encouraging people speak positive things into our lives. While there were those who spoke encouragement, there were also those who spoke judgment. "God must be upset with you two about something. Can you think of what it is?" Because of the latter, it made us want to be alone and not be bothered with anyone.

In the book *Compassionate Care* by John W. Walton, when speaking to spiritual care providers, he gives some very enlightening advice for those ministering to the sick, dying or hurting which I think would have been quite beneficial to my wife and me during our time of crisis. "Expect anything! Let nothing surprise you. Nevertheless, when you are present, just 'be' there! Pray and let your sixth sense show you what the needs are" (Walton, 2007, p 83).

I do not believe everyone has the heart to minister to individuals in certain situations. I have learned throughout the years whenever I visit someone who is grieving, the best thing I can do is listen to him or her. If you listen long and hard enough, you will be able to hear their pain and know what to pray for them about, and not just spend time ineffectively talking.

We did not want to speak with anyone or see anyone. All we wanted to do was to be alone. Many of those who did try to comfort us often said the wrong thing and ended up making us feel worse rather than better.

I remember a quote I had recently read, that summed up many of our feelings during our loss:

"You probably feel quite overwhelmed and bewildered right now, sort of like you were picked up and placed on a different planet! This grief thing is a surreal new world of uncharted territory for you, and no one gave you a roadmap" ("Grief Loss Recovery," para. 5).

Chapter 14
THE BABY SHOWER

After the loss of our son, a pastor friend of mine invited my wife and me to come to Tennessee and spend some time just to get away. He put us up in a nice hotel and told us we could just relax and take it easy if we wanted to. He said if we did not feel up to coming to church, that would be all right with him.

The trip to Tennessee was a welcomed invitation, as we had been dealing with so much and just needed to be in a different environment.

We decided that going to church and hearing the message would be uplifting for the both of us. The message encouraged us and made us feel much better. Things were going well and after service, there was an announcement that one of the young women in the church was having a baby shower at the church at 4:00pm immediately after service. They invited my wife to come. This was quite emotional for her; this was the first baby shower that Shirley had received an invitation to since the loss of our son. The invitation to the baby shower triggered emotions that we had just recently tried to bury. We realized at that time, these strong emotions had not yet died and would be with us for a long time.

I can still remember the look on my wife's face as she tried to be supportive of the new mother and child. I could, however, see the sadness and hurt in her eyes as if this was another reminder of our recent loss. All I could do was be there for her. You would think that with me being a pastor and always comforting others in their time of grief, I would know just what to say, that I would have plenty of words to encourage my own wife who I could see was clearly hurting. However, I was at a loss for words, I was speechless. It was as though I was numb; maybe it was because I was hurting just as bad as she was, but once again, I had to be strong for her. I had to dismiss my own hurt and comfort my wife who needed the support I was able to give her so desperately.

As I embraced my wife telling her everything was going to be all right, I was still secretly questioning God. For years, I remembered being taught as a child, you should not question God. Still I had questions, and I was not getting any answers. Was everything really going to be all right? How could I be sure things were *really* going to be all right? Did I even believe what I was saying to her? Was I just saying this to make Shirley feel better or did I believe what I was saying?

My wife asked me to take her to the store to purchase a gift for the new mother, but she was not emotionally able to attend the shower. I remember going back to our hotel room and just holding my wife; telling her everything was going to be all right and we would somehow get through this together.

Chapter 15
INSENSITIVITY FROM OTHERS

After the death of our son, I was amazed and appalled by many of the things said to my wife and me. While there were many who were supportive, others just did not know exactly what to say, as well as those who just did not care. For those who were at a loss for words, I could understand, but for those who spoke in ignorance, at times, I must say it was hard for me to overlook them, thinking they should know better.

I remember when someone overheard me speaking about our son to another individual; they just could not understand why Shirley and I were grieving. They interjected into a conversation that I was having with this other person and stated, "I don't know why you just don't move on? He was just a baby," as if because he was not an adult that it really should not have mattered, that we should not be upset over his loss. It was unbelievable the things that were told to Shirley and me after just losing our baby.

There were others who tried to encourage us by saying things like, "Don't worry you two will have another," implying that we should not grieve over the loss of our son, but just move on. It was just not that easy for us. We had a son, we watched him grow, we became attached to him, and now he had been taken away from us. We could not go on as if he had never lived.

Going Back to Work (More Insensitivity)

I struggled as to whether I should include this part in this book, but as I stated at the beginning, my desire is to be frank and honest about our experiences before, during and after the loss of our child. I pray that no one else who has suffered any type of loss like the one we have will ever have to deal with this type of insensitivity and outright cruelness.

I finally had to go back to work, even though I really did not want to. Just as at church, I did not want to have to answer a whole lot of questions. All I wanted to do when asked questions regarding our son, was to just say nothing, smile and go about my day. I took medical leave off from work, and this was my first day back on the job. After being at work for about an hour, my boss calls me into her office.

I am thinking my boss is calling me into her office to see how I was doing, but that was not the case. She called me into her office to inform me that because of the amount of time I had taken off, I was in jeopardy of being suspended or, worse yet, losing my job. I am thinking to myself, this cannot really be happening to me. How insensitive can you be?

When I thought it could not get any worse, my supervisor now tells me her boss wants to talk with me in her office. My manager's boss proceeds to tell me, "This is a business and I know you have a lot going on but we are expecting you to be here." I am hurt and angry by now, but it gets worse. I tell my boss that due to the loss of our child, I had to take time off with my wife. My boss never once says, "I'm sorry for your loss." What she says next is unbelievable. "You knew your wife couldn't have children, before you got her pregnant. Maybe you all should just quit trying." I thought to myself, thank God I am a Christian because there are any number of ways I could react to what she just said. I kept my composure, because I knew if I had responded like I felt, it would have gotten ugly in that office that day.

After I got back to my desk, I was still very upset but remained quiet. My immediate supervisor (not her boss) calls me back to her office again and informs me that, after looking over my record a second time that they acted too hastily in responding to my absences. "Tony, I'm sorry, we made a mistake. You are not in any trouble with your attendance. We miscalculated your days off. Your attendance is fine." It was unbelievable that they put me through all that on my first day back to work for nothing. However, I knew they were hoping that my attendance was bad. I actually thought about retaliating but two scriptures came to mind:

"Wherefore, my beloved brethren, let every man be swift to hear, slow to speak, slow to wrath" (James 1:19, King James Version)

"Be ye angry, and sin not: let not the sun go down upon your wrath" (Ephesians 4:26, King James Version)

Millard Fuller, Founder and President Habitat for Humanity International writes about not fighting problems, but solving them. He talks about how to effectively deal with negative situations. After speaking with my boss, I admit that I was enraged. I did not quite know how to respond. My first thought was to share some words with her that I had not used in over eleven years. My second thought was to quit, but the spirit of God convicted me, and I realized that would not solve the problem, but actually make things worse. That would probably even make them happy to see me quit.

Fuller tells of a story about speaking with a person who was unhappy with their workplace and ended up resigning, as I felt like doing. He questioned a person after hearing of their resignation by asking, "I mean, did your resignation accomplish anything other than getting you out of the picture? Did your leaving make things better for the people you cared for so much?" Later, he advises them to consider solutions rather than fighting the problem (Fuller, 2002, p 20).

Whenever you are dealing with grief, often there is the feeling of anger, which can cause you to react to stressful situations in a different manner than if you were not experiencing anxiety. I learned to think before I react or speak. By doing this, I was able to get over the anger against my boss and move forward. I realized it was not about her, but about me allowing God to take control of my life.

Chapter 16
THE GRIEF/ANNIVERSARIES/BIRTH-DEATH

According to the American Association for Marriage and Family Therapy (AAMFT). "The loss of a child is the most devastating experience a parent can face, and missing the child never goes away. A piece of yourself is lost and your future is forever changed" (Weiss, n.d. 2000).

Many counselors note - and from the personal experiences my wife and I had, we can relate to this, can be a lonely period in their lives. We could hardly speak to anyone. We just wanted to be left alone. We felt as though no one could understand what we were going through. We experienced a wide range of emotions, but if it wasn't for the grace of God, there is no telling where our mixed emotions would have taken us.

However, the two of us dealt with the grief differently. She was more open and expressive about hers, where I tended to suffer in silence. Often times, I wonder if I have really ever truly dealt completely with my grief. I believe writing this book is part of my personal journey toward complete healing for myself.

According to many experts, the pain never completely goes away. For many who have experienced this hurt, time helps, but it does not erase the pain. Throughout the years, Shirley and I, at times, were at a loss of words for each other. It was completely overwhelming. We would look at each other as though we wanted to say something, but the words just could not come out. We both knew that the other was hurting and all we could do was to be there for each other to lean on.

Prior to losing our son, my wife had suffered a number of miscarriages as well. While we were slowly beginning to overcome those hurts, we now had to face what was to be an even greater challenge and hurt.

In the book *When Your Whole World Changes*, there is this quote: "When I think about the disaster – the people who died, the wrecked homes – I start questioning everything I wonder about the purpose of life in general. Life can be so cruel."

"For God so loved the world that he gave his only begotten Son, that whosoever believeth in him should not perish, but have everlasting life. For God sent not his Son into the world to condemn the world; but that the world through him might be saved."
(John 3:16-17, King James Version)

This scripture is one that gives us the hope, that the love of God stands for and is available to all those who will accept it.

Every year I never forget the date of my son's birth as well as that awful sad day when we had to lay him to rest. In all of the years since his passing, I have only been able to look at the pictures we took of him about three times.

There was a woman I worked with who also suffered the loss of her infant son. She kept a picture of him on her desk at work to look at every day. For me, this would have been unbearable for me to look at my son's picture every day. People grieve in different ways; this was her way of dealing with his loss.

SEVEN STAGES OF GRIEF –
Through the Process and Back to Life

- Shock & Denial
- Pain & Guilt
- Anger & Bargaining
- "Depression: Reflection, Loneliness
- The Upward turn
- Reconstruction & Working Through
- Acceptance & Hope

Author Angela Miller

Chapter 17
THE ACCEPTING OF GOD'S WILL

The accepting of God's will for our life is often a very difficult task for anyone, especially when it goes against what we want or desire for ourselves and for those whom we love and care for.

"By little and little I will drive them out from before thee, until thou be increased, and inherit the land"
(*Exodus 23:30, King James Version*)

Overcoming any challenge is difficult. Drug, addictions, alcoholism, depression, the loss of a child, and any other kind of loss often requires a long and hard fought process. This is a day-by-day process. We do not always know why God takes us on the paths He does, but we know that just like He took the children of Israel from the wilderness to the Promised Land, it is sometimes a slow and tedious journey. Overcoming pain and hurt are never instantaneous, but is normally a process where we must learn to trust in God, believing we will come out.

My faith was totally dependent on God to get me out of the slump I was in. I had to define who I was in God. I had to realize something: God did not allow this to happen to me because he was angry with me, but there had to be a divine reason for this. I had to remind myself that God still loved Shirley and me, and whatever situations he was taking us through, the reason we were still standing was his love, his mercy, and his grace.

Josh McDowell defines a healthy self-image as, "Seeing yourself as God sees you-no more and no less" (McDowell, 1984). I could not allow myself to look at Shirley and me as though we were the victims of our circumstances, even though we were going through a great storm. Rather, we were children of God. We had the assurance we would be comforted and protected by His love.

The reason I am mostly focusing on me at this time is that before I could help Shirley, I had to deal with and overcome my own personal and individual hurt in order to be able to help her or anyone else to overcome their struggles.

I had to realize and identify all the things that were going on in my life that were positive. Many times, we focus on the negative things going on in our lives instead of thanking God for the blessings he has already given us. If we continue to look back, and allow ourselves to only focus on the hurts of our past, we will never see the great opportunities God has in store for our future as we look forward in hopes of a better tomorrow.

"I had fainted, unless I had believed to see the goodness of the Lord in the land of the living."
(Psalms 27:13, King James Version)

If we view only the negative and not the good things in life, we will find ourselves in a continuous state of depression.

"Finally, brethren, whatsoever things are true, whatsoever things are honest, whatsoever things are just, whatsoever things are pure, whatsoever things are lovely, whatsoever things are of good report; if there be any virtue, and if there be any praise, think on these things."
(Philippians 4:8, King James Version)

"And it came to pass on the seventh day that the child died. And the servants of David feared to tell him that the child was dead: for they said, Behold, while the child was yet alive, we spake unto him, and he would not hearken unto our voices: how will he then vex himself if we tell him that the child is dead?"
(2 Samuel 12:18, King James Version)

When it comes to accepting the will of God regarding any kind of a loss, most of us deal with loss in different ways. People will tell you, "If I were you, I would have handled it like this or that." However, each person is different and everyone deals with his or her loss in the best way he or she knows how, depending on his or her worldview. They often draw from their personal life experiences and support systems. The greater the amount of life experiences to draw from and the greater their support systems, the more likely they are to have the ability to effectively deal with their challenges. Some people feel that, taking their problems to God in prayer is the answer. While I agree this is what we should do as Christians, I must admit it is not as easy as it sounds when you are in the midst of your pain, at least for most of us.

Probably one of the worst ways of dealing with our hurt is through extended periods of isolation. There are times when it is good to be alone, and yet there are times when you need the encouragement and support of others to help see you through.

"But when David saw that his servants whispered, David perceived that the child was dead: therefore, David said unto his servants, is the child dead? And they said He is dead. Then David arose from the earth, and washed, and anointed himself, and changed his apparel, and came into the house of the Lord, and worshiped: then he came to his own house and when he required, they set bread before him, and he did eat."
(*2 Samuel 12:19-20, King James Version*)

This is not the normal response to the loss of a child. David went from one extreme to another. You can never predict how a person will handle grief.

David did not go through the usual grieving process when he lost his child as many of us do. In other parts of his life, we see where he dealt with his pain in a very different way. However, there are times when we see David calling out to God in anguish over his situations.

"Why art thou cast down, O my soul? And why art thou disquieted within me? Hope thou in God: for I shall yet praise him, for the help of his countenance"
(Psalms 42:5, King James Version)

"My God, my God, why hast thou forsaken me? why art thou so far from helping me, and from the words of my roaring? O my God, I cry in the day time, but thou hearest not; and in the night season, and am not silent."
(Psalms 22:1-2, King James Version)

Chapter 18
SHOULD WE TRY AGAIN TO HAVE ANOTHER CHILD?

After the death of our son, we were faced with the dilemma of whether or not we would try to have another child. We asked ourselves if we could handle the pain and hurt that we experienced with the birth and death of our son.

After many talks, counseling with others, and much prayer, we decided that we would try to have another child. It was about nine months after the death of our son. We felt we were now emotionally ready to have another child. We had prayed about it and felt the time was right.

Shirley was now pregnant, and after about three months she went into early labor again. It was as if we were reliving the same bad nightmare over again. We found ourselves in the same situation as before.

I can remember sitting in the waiting room with my friend Kevin Davenport waiting to hear the news from the doctor as to the status of Shirley's condition. I remember Kevin telling me, "I don't think God will allow this to happen to you again." I so wanted to believe he was right.

Then, the doctor told us that this baby would definitely not make it through the delivery. I said, "I still have faith the baby can make it." He again confirmed by stating, "The baby will definitely not make it through the delivery this time." My wife had the baby (a little girl) and we could hear her crying. The doctor took the girl from Shirley and turned his back toward us. The next thing he said to us was that she was dead. Once again, we were devastated over the death of our child. We always wondered if the doctor had done something to cause the death of our child. As the doctor moved away from Shirley and me with the baby, we saw what appeared to be a jerking motion from him. A motion as if someone was ringing a rag. Shirley and I both wondered if maybe he had tried to play God in order to spare us from what he thought would be the pain of us going through what we had experienced during her previous birth. We will never know the answer to that question, but through the years, we have always wondered about that. Even the nurse that was in the room expressed her concerns over what she had seen, letting us know that she felt the same way as we did regarding the doctors' action.

There were those who encouraged us to believe in God and not give up, but at the same time, there were almost as many of those who discouraged us and said, all of this was too much physically and emotionally for Shirley to handle.

One of the first things we did was to change Shirley's gynecologist. I was never happy with her original doctor from the first time I met him. Shirley and I checked around for a different doctor. The doctor referred to us seemed kind and understanding from the time we met him. I was pleased with him from the first time we met. This doctor told us that he would do his best to see that Shirley would be able to deliver a healthy baby. Shirley and I both found that to be very reassuring. He had Shirley take a number of tests and said he would get back with us on the results.

After all the testing, the doctor was certain of the source of the problem. The problem was that my wife had an incompetent cervix, also called a "cervical insufficiency." This is a condition that occurs when weak cervical tissue causes or contributes to premature birth or the loss of an otherwise healthy pregnancy (Mayo Foundation for Medical Education and Research, 2016).

Once we were aware of the problem, we were able to monitor Shirley's progress, allowing us to be proactive in the birth and delivery of our next child. We found out that because of my wife's diagnosis, there would be the possibility she would be bedridden for a period of time during her pregnancy. She was more than willing to make that sacrifice.

Chapter 19
I'M PREGNANT AGAIN!

After about twelve years of marriage and approximately six of those years actively wanting and trying to have a child, we were excited to hear the news that my wife was pregnant again. We were excited, because we now knew what Shirley would have to do to avoid the previous losses. We began to share the good news with all our family and friends about her being pregnant. Her being pregnant received mixed reviews from family and friends. Shirley was excited, I was excited, and some of our friends, and family were excited along with us to hear the good news. However, there were those negative persons who expressed their thoughts that this was not a good idea.

Our next goal was that of getting the house ready for our new arrival. We picked out the room and decided it was time to get the baby furniture. I let Shirley decide what she wanted, and where she wanted to get it. I went along with her some of the time whenever she would ask me to, but mostly, I would let her shop with her sisters for many of the items.

By this time, Shirley was about five to six months pregnant and everything was looking good. She picked out the baby furniture, gotten it at home and was making plans for our new arrival. She had now begun to purchase baby clothes. We did not know if we were going to have a boy or a girl. We wanted it to be a surprise, so we bought clothes that the baby could wear whether it was a girl or a boy.

Every day, Shirley would do something different preparing for the arrival of our new baby. There was such a feeling of excitement as we both were looking forward to the sounds of a newborn in our home.

Everything was going well for my wife during this pregnancy. However, entering into her eighth week, she started having complications again. We went to the doctor and he suggested that my wife have a procedure done called a "cervical cerclage." This procedure uses stitches to close the cervix during pregnancy to help prevent pregnancy loss or premature birth (Mayo Foundation for Medical Education and Research, 2016).

During this time as my wife and I went through this next ordeal, we learned more medical terms than we both cared to know. However, it gave us some comfort and a little more insight into what was going on, because we now knew about the major problem my wife was having, and why our son and daughter were both born prematurely.

At about eight weeks into the pregnancy, she started spotting, needless to say, we were very concerned. Our anxiety levels started to go up once again. We were afraid that we would have the same experience as we had gone through before. We immediately contacted her doctor, and he suggested that we get into his office as soon as possible. Again, we did not know exactly what to think. We thought we were past all of this.

After seeing, the doctor and having the doctor to check her out completely, our concerns were alleviated. The doctor assured us that Shirley would be all right, but to be on the safe side, he suggested that she be bedridden for a few weeks. We learned that because her cervix was weak, it could not hold the weight of the baby as it grew to be bigger, and that was why she would go into early labor. This was the problem she was having earlier.

Things were going well until about sixteen weeks into her pregnancy, and she again started having problems. It was so frustrating. We again called the doctor, and he advised us that Shirley would have to have an additional surgery. This surgery would be a little different from the first surgery. This surgery is called an "umbilical cerclage". When bulging prolapsed membranes develop out of the cervix into the vagina during the second trimester, in many cases the situation progresses to abortion or premature birth, and neonatal prognosis is poor. Since neonatal prognosis is affected by the number of weeks of gestation, the prolongation of gestation is generally attempted for as long as possible. It is difficult to extend the pregnancy period by conservative therapy, however, and keeping the mother resting in bed for a long time increases the risk of thrombosis and infection (Kanai, Ashida, Ohira, Osadaand, and Konish, 2008).

Shirley and I felt like we were riding on an emotional roller coaster. Just when we thought things were settling down, something else would happen. We tried our best to maintain a positive attitude.

We knew our friends and family, and even those who did not care for us were watching us to see what kind of an attitude we were having. There were those who would come up to us and say, "Boy, things are looking pretty rough, aren't they?" We would just look at them, smile, and say, "We're going to be alright!" We would try our best to maintain a positive attitude. "Sometimes our attitudes can be masked outwardly and others who see us are fooled. But usually the cover-ups will not last long" (Maxwell, 2003, p 13).

We found that during these difficult times, it was a challenge to keep ourselves motivated, as we still had to maintain our daily responsibilities. We could not just allow ourselves to focus on our problems and end up sinking into depression or lose hope, but we chose to keep the faith and trust that God was in control and everything somehow would work out for our good.

Whenever we found ourselves to be at a low point, we would remind each other of the scripture:

"And we know that all things work together for good to them that love God, to them who are the called according to his purpose."
(Romans 8:28, King James Version)

Chapter 20
THOUGHT FOR PASTORS ON MOTHER'S DAY/FATHER'S DAY

I remember during the times when my wife so dearly wanted a child, it was hard for her to go to church on Mother's Day. She had gotten to the place where it became so difficult that sometimes she could not bear the emotional pain and would choose not to attend services at all that day. Pastors often gloat over the mothers on Mother's Day, and I can certainly understand why they would do this. Mothers are so special and not only deserve one day of recognition, but should be recognized for all the many acts of kindness and sacrifices they make for their families, day in and day out, on a continuous basis. My experience with my wife, dealing with her grief, not being able to be recognized as a mother, circumstances beyond her control, the death of our child – all of this caused me to rethink how I address the mothers on Mother's Day. I recognize <u>all</u> the women in the church, whether they are biological mothers or not. I recognize there are many women in the church who have never been able to birth a natural child for one reason or another, but possess the spirit of a loving, caring, and nurturing mother.

I encourage pastors to be considerate also of the men in their congregations who may not be able to have a child for the same reasons. I do this without taking away from the spirit of the occasion.

Pastors and others may not be aware of the pain resulting from the loss of, or inability to have, a child that those in their congregations may feel on this special holiday. These individuals, while smiling on the outside, are many times filled with pain and hurt on the inside.

Every biological parent does not always possess the spirit of a mother or a father. There are those individuals to whom God has given a true spirit of a father or mother and can often be seen nurturing and caring for others, as if they were their own children, biological or not. These are the individuals I recognize and salute on Mother's and Father's Day.

Chapter 21
IT'S A GIRL!

One day, while my wife and I were at church, an older mother in the church about eighty-seven years of age came to my wife and me and started to laugh. She said some show it here, pointing to my wife's stomach, and some show it there, pointing to her backside. We did not think much of it. We thought she was referring to Shirley picking up weight or she was just sort of rambling. It was all so random. She just laughed and we laughed just to amuse her. Little did we know that older mother was in tune with the Spirit of God and nature. We did not know it yet, but this older mother was actually trying to tell us what we were waiting to hear for years - that my wife was pregnant.

That same week, my wife had her regular doctor's appointment. Even though we often thought about having a child, part of us accepted the fact that we would not be able to have children and part of us continued hoping for a miracle. My wife had gone for her yearly check-up and not expecting to hear what the doctor told her. "Congratulations, you're going to be a mother!"

When Shirley got home, she could not wait to share the good news with me. This is the news we had been waiting for, for so long. As we talked about her pregnancy, we reflected on what the mother at church had shared with us just a week prior. We realized that this is what she had been referring to on that Sunday.

Five years after the loss of our son, my wife again was pleased to find out she was expecting another child. Due to the complications my wife had with her previous pregnancy, we were excited; however, we naturally experienced some trepidation regarding the possible birth of our child.

I was vigilant to see that Shirley did not stress herself or put herself in any position that would cause any harm to the baby or place any undue stress on her that would affect the baby. I spoiled and pampered her the entire time. Her every wish was my command! I believe Shirley relished every minute of it.

Chapter 22
MAKING IT TO THIRTY-TWO WEEKS

The doctor assured us that everything was going well. The doctor gave us a target date of thirty-two weeks. During the pregnancy, it felt as if I were having the baby too! We were in this together. My wife would tease me because sometimes I would wake up with morning sickness. This was likely due to the amount of stress and anxiety we both were experiencing during this time. Shirley would make fun of me and say, "Who's having this baby, you or me?" If we could just make it to thirty-two weeks, we would be in the safe zone.

Every day, week, and month we made it through brought her closer to the point where the doctor felt it would be safer for the baby's delivery. We would celebrate each new month that she made it through, not taking anything for granted. Something that so many people take for granted, we would celebrate. It would be another milestone for us to mark. Every month would be one-step closer to our baby being born.

Because the doctor monitored Shirley so closely, we learned this time we were going to have a girl. Our only desire was to have a healthy child. That was our main concern, that and making sure Shirley remained healthy throughout her pregnancy.

As we got closer to the date of Shirley having the baby, there was still a lot of anxiety and apprehension about whether or not she would be able to carry the baby for the entire thirty-two weeks. Whenever she would feel the slightest discomfort, it made us afraid of what could possibly happen next. We could never forget our previous experiences and did not want to experience them again.

Many nights Shirley could not sleep, so to pass the time we would often play a card game called "Uno" or another game called "Connect Four." We played for hours and hours every night. We sometimes played until one and two o'clock in the morning. (I am convinced that is the reason our daughter likes to stay up late to this day.) She brags that no one can beat her at "Connect Four." I believe that is because she could hear me beating her mom at that game while she was still in the womb. Playing these games into the wee hours of the morning gave Shirley something to do on those many restless nights when she was unable to sleep. It also was a time of bonding for the two of us. It gave us time to reflect on our experiences as well as a chance to share our thoughts and goals for our future with our newborn.

An Evangelist name Mildred Boyd, knowing we wanted to have a child, would often pray for us. I remember her saying in her raspy voice from preaching so hard, "We going to h-a-v-e this baby!" She said it with such faith and confidence that it would strengthen our faith every time she would say it. We had periods where our faith was very strong and then there were times when our faith would be challenged.

Many of our friends near and far knew what all we had been through and they would often call us or send us a message with an encouraging word. Often they would tell us that everything was going to be all right. We so much needed to hear these expressions of encouragement, as each word seemed to help to lift our faith. We so desperately wanted to believe that everything was going to be all right.

I was taking my last class at my undergrad school and a classmate of mine knew my wife was expecting. She asked me if this was our first child. This was always a sensitive subject. I did not want to go into a long story and have to rehash what Shirley and I had gone through, so I would respond to them by keeping it simple and just saying, "Yes." However, on this occasion, I did share with her our previous experience.

A few weeks later, my classmate told me she had a baby present for Shirley and me. I thought how nice. This was our first gift for our baby. I felt funny because I began to think of what had happened before. Will we have to give it back? She said she believed everything was going to be all right. It was a pink ceramic light switch with a baby girl on it. It was so special to us. I really was afraid to put it up. I guess this was just the trick of the enemy causing me to think putting the switch in her room would cause something bad to happen. Shirley and I talked about it and decided we would put it up by faith. We still have it to this day.

"For God hath not given us the spirit of fear; but of power, and of love, and of a sound mind."
(2 Timothy 1:7, King James Version)

As we got closer to the time of her delivery, it was nearing the end of December. Because of the previous surgery Shirley had to prevent her cervix from opening up, the doctor informed us that she would have to have the baby delivered by cesarean. He also gave us the option of picking the date in which the baby would be born. We chose January 15, a date we knew neither of us would ever forget. It was also on the closest weekend and Shirley was ready to deliver the baby by now. After all she had gone through, it seemed like it had been a long time since she first found out she was pregnant.

Because so many were aware of our previous losses, we had so many people praying and rooting for us. On my job, they told me to make sure I called the office just as soon as the baby was born.

Chapter 23
THE DAY BEFORE THE DELIVERY

It was January 14, 1993. Shirley and I were getting more and more excited. We would tell each other, "Just think, this time tomorrow we will have a little baby girl!" By this time, we had found out that we were having a girl. We prepared for and made everything ready for the new arrival. We had the bedroom decorated with all kinds of furniture and baby toys, much of which was given to Shirley at the many baby showers she had been given.

The evangelist who prayed for us called me the night before we were scheduled to go to the hospital and requested that I pick her up to go to the hospital to be with us during the delivery. I told her, I would be glad to pick her up. We had to be at the hospital by 6:30 a.m., so I told her we would pick her up at about 5:30 a.m.

That night, my wife and I could hardly sleep, so we did what we had been doing for the previous 4-5 months, playing "Uno" and "Connect Four" until we both got tired and made ourselves go to bed. We knew the next day would be a long and busy day for us, so we decided Shirley should get some rest.

Chapter 24
THE DAY OF THE DELIVERY

It was Friday, January 15, 1993 – the day we had been waiting for, for so long. We got up very early. We could hardly sleep the night before because of the anticipation. We got up early that morning and prayed, we asked God "please let everything go smoothly". Shirley had already packed her things and was ready for the trip to the hospital. We were so excited, we both knew when we would return home from the hospital, our lives would never be the same from that day forward, for better or for worse.

As we prayed, we agreed to put our faith into action. We refused to think on anything negative at this time. We began to rehearse many of the scriptures that we had heard and recited from the past.

We were both optimistic about the outcome of this trip to the hospital. We had many visits to the hospital before, but this time was very different. Things were looking good and we were trusting in God.

Taking Extra Precautions

When we got to the hospital, they ran the usual tests and a few extra ones just as a precaution due to Shirley's past medical history. As we got closer and closer, not only were we concerned about the baby, but about Shirley's health. Earlier, I mentioned how what many other women take for granted we could not. We were aware that a number of women die each year during childbirth and this was a concern for the both of us.

"In 2015, an estimated 303,000 women will die from complications related to pregnancy or childbirth. In addition, for every woman who dies in childbirth, dozens more suffer injury, infection or disease" (World Health Organization, 2015).

We also knew that, while many individuals take having a C-section for granted, that, too, also comes with a certain amount of risk. According to the American Pregnancy Association, there are a number of risks when delivering a baby by C-section. "More than 1 in 4 women are likely to experience a cesarean delivery." Some of the risks are infections, hemorrhaging, scarring, and longer hospital stays. There is also risks for the baby, such as premature births (American Pregnancy Association, 2015).

Chapter 25
SHE'S HERE!

It was approximately five years after the loss of our son, and we were again in the waiting room expecting another child. Due to the complications my wife had with her previous pregnancy, we were excited but had some apprehension about the birth of our child.

I tried to maintain an attitude and atmosphere of nothing but positive thoughts. Everyone there was upbeat and careful to see that Shirley did not allow herself to become too stressed out.

This was the big day we had all been waiting for. I say "all" because what happened to Shirley and I affected so many people. After running the various tests, the doctor asked us if we were ready. What a question! Were we ready? We had been ready for this day for over nine years! This is what we prayed for, what others prayed for. This was the big day.

The doctors and nurses were very upbeat. We were in the same hospital where we lost our son five years earlier. A number of the same staff still working there and were aware of our previous losses. It was as if everyone was optimistically but cautiously waiting and anticipating the birth of our child.

The nurse came to get Shirley to get her ready, and told me they would bring me back in a few minutes. As I waited, what was only minutes, seemed like hours! I anxiously waited for the nurse to come back and get me.

Finally, the nurse came and got me. As I was walking down the hall on my way to meet Shirley, my mind began to race over the events of our lives, some of the ups and downs, the hurts and pain, but I was rejoicing because through everything we had gone through, we made it. We managed to stay together, we managed to keep our sanity, and we managed to keep our faith, (even though many times it wavered). Yet, regardless of what the outcome of the next few minutes would be, I had a feeling that everything was going to come out right. Yes, everything was going to be just fine.

As I met with Shirley and the doctor, he was very upbeat and so was Shirley. One thing I thought was funny was when the doctor took his hands, and as if he was holding a football out in front of him, began moving his hands and showing us that just by looking at Shirley he could guess the weight and length of the baby. He gave a prediction off the top of his head, and when our baby was born, he was completely accurate.

Now it was time for the procedure. I was not in any way nervous to be in the delivery room. I had my video camera on hand to video this special occasion. Shirley was not too happy about this at first, but at this point, she was willing to go along with anything just to have the procedure over. I made certain that the video was discrete, capturing only the baby. I asked Shirley, "Are you ready?" She said, "Are you kidding?" The doctor said, "Here we go!" It was not long before we heard the melodious sounds of a screaming little baby girl.

The smile on my wife's face as she held our daughter for the first time was priceless. Her entire facial expression seemed to change at that moment. She seemed to be beaming with the excitement of having a new baby, of becoming a new mom. Finally, blessed to have a healthy child, was such a joy! We knew at that time, and we now know, that our daughter was and continues to be a blessing from God. We consider her our miracle baby. People from all over the world were praying for her safe entry into the world. Even today, I go places and people will ask about her and tell me they remember what all Shirley and I went through.

I went into the waiting room and shared the good news with our friends and family who had gotten up early that morning to support us during the birth of our daughter. They were all excited and you could hear it all the way down the hall! Ethel Walton (my mother), Evangelist Mildred Boyd, Jacquelyn Coleman, Mother Anita Johnson, and Brenda Radford all rejoiced with us in this long-awaited blessing.

Next given an order by my co-workers to call them as soon as the baby was born. I called the office and they answered the phone on the first ring. They were nervously waiting to hear from us. They were all waiting to hear the good news. I told them we had a healthy baby girl. Before I could say anything else, the person who I was talking with repeated, "It's a healthy baby girl!" I could hear them cheering in the background.

Later on, while we were in our private room, we were surprised to have a visit by the doctor who had attended to our son five years earlier. She was so excited for us; she began to cry and share tears of joy for what God had done for us. We were reflecting on the memories of our son, appreciating what all we had been through, and grateful for how we were able to overcome all the challenges of the loss of our son.

As we looked back on the journey that God chose to take us on, it caused us to grow closer to each other as a couple, to learn to accept the will of God, and to learn to appreciate others and the "little things" in life that others take for granted. We now see that at the end of our journey of desiring to have a baby, our daughter, Christina Alisha Walton, was a gift from God. She has been and still is a blessing to Shirley and me.

Chapter 26
THE SHARING OF YOUR LOSS WITH OTHERS

"Compassion and love, not advice, are needed"
Author Angela Miller

Author Angela Miller writes in "A Bed for My Heart", that there were seven things she learned after the loss of her child.

- Love never dies
- Bereaved parents share an unbreakable bond
- I will grieve for a lifetime
- It's a club I can never leave, but is filled with the most shining souls I've ever known.
- The empty chair/room/space never becomes less empty
- No matter how long it has been, holidays never become easier without my son
- Because I know deep sorrow, I also know unspeakable joy

For some time, I was unable to talk with anyone about what was going on with me, about how I was feeling during our loss. I think part of the reason was because of the negative reactions of those with whom I had previously spoken before. A number of them seem to minimize the loss we had experienced. This caused me to want to retreat within myself, and not share any of my feelings with others.

The process of being able to share your grief with others, for many of those who have experienced the loss of a loved one, is not always an easy one. For many, they keep their feelings locked up inside of them. I am one of those who, for a long time, kept everything bottled up inside of me. Even today, I still feel there is a part of me that has not completely healed from the memories and the pain of our loss. A slow process, which you cannot rush.

Often people make the mistake of not understanding why a person does not move forward in their lives and go past their present feelings. I have heard it said to others as well as myself, "Why don't you just hurry up and get over it, and move on with your life?"

The ability to share your hurt is the beginning of the healing process; however, you cannot make a person open up to you and talk about their loss until they are ready to, until the time is right for them.

Couples grieve together as well as individually. They both have to experience their own individual and personal journeys. As you are able to overcome your personal journey, then you are better able to help your mate to overcome and go through their journey.

Dr. Glenn Mollette, in his book *Silent Struggler*, speaks about how he felt he was ready to move on after the death of his and his wife's son. He was ready to move on after the funeral. "Let's put the death of this baby behind us." He was trying to get his wife to focus on what they had, rather than the loss they experienced. Everyone moves at his or her own pace.

Dr. Mollette states, "It is impossible in a marriage relationship to go forward by yourself. To go forward and accomplish anything, both partners need to be going in the same direction" (Mollette, 2000, p 9).

From my personal experience, if both partners are not going in the same direction, there will be little peace and harmony. The couples must decide to grow together, even if it involves taking baby steps. One person may find himself or herself having to slow down and take note of what the other person is dealing with. After all, what joy will you have making it to the finish line alone without your mate? The goal should be the unity of the relationship and finding peace and making it to the finish line together.

As I became stronger in God and allowed my faith in God to grow, I was able then, and even more so now, to share with others how Shirley and I overcame a very difficult time in our life by not giving up on my faith. Our faith was tested, but we refused through all the hurt and pain to give up on God. We realized if God could not help Shirley and me through this journey, then no one else could.

There was a pastor's daughter who went through many of the same experiences that Shirley went through. She thought she would not be able to have a child. After many years of her trying unsuccessfully to have a child, just like Shirley and I had previously gone through, she was about to give up. After talking with Shirley and allowing her to minister with her by sharing her personal testimony, as well as referring the pastor's daughter to the doctor who treated Shirley, the young woman was blessed to be able to have a beautiful, healthy baby girl.

"Expressing concerns and empathizing with others provides hope. Empathizing with others also brings continued healing to the comforter" (Frank, 1995).

On one occasion, while I was ministering in the state of Michigan, as I was extending the call to discipleship, a young woman came down the aisle, crying and sobbing uncontrollably. I could see how she was all broken up. She began to share with me how she had just lost her child and felt no one had any idea of how she was feeling or about what she was going through. I was able to minister to her from my personal experience, from my pain, from the hurt Shirley and I had gone through. Although our situations were not exactly the same. She was comforted in knowing someone else had gone through some of the same similar circumstances of what she had gone through and was able to overcome it.

To this day, I do not know why Shirley and I had to go through what we did. I have asked God many times, but I have come to learn and understand there are some things in this life we will never understand, but we will have to continue to trust and believe in God by faith.

Chapter 27
THE LITTLE RED WAGON

I was told of a true story of a mother who had a child. The mother, after giving birth, had to be admitted to the hospital. The father was not able to care for the child because his previous four children overwhelmed him. In those days, families and neighbors were much closer than they are today. This was before internet and cable TV. During those times, you would sit on your porch and talk with your family and often a neighbor would just drop by for a friendly conversation.

There was a woman in the neighborhood who was unable to have a child, and heard about the father's dilemma and sent someone to inquire if she could take the baby in. The father, because of his circumstances, agreed to let the neighbor take the child. After getting word that the father would allow her to raise the child, she then sent two of the kids in the neighborhood with a little red wagon to pick the child up. Because they lived so close together, the mother and father were able to see the child every day.

My reason for including this story is that too many mothers, rather than choosing to give their child away, they choose the option of killing their baby. I would like to encourage anyone who knows of a mother who, for whatever reason, does not feel that they can handle the burden of raising a child to consider other options. Many couples out there would love to parent an unwanted child, even if they have to bring a little red wagon to the mother's house to pick it up.

Chapter 28
YOU ARE NOT ALONE!

After many years of grieving, my wife and I came to realize that we were not suffering alone. Many individuals suffer having to deal with the experience of losing a child, for whatever reason and at whatever age. The pain is often still there, and the pain is very real.

I spoke with a couple who lost a child some years prior. As we spoke, tears began to run down the eyes of the father as he thought and talked about his child. Getting over the loss of a child is never easy. It is a lifelong process. You never really get over it, but rather, you learn to accept the loss as you keep the memory of your loved one in your heart forever.

There are many heart wrenching stories that others have shared with me throughout the years over the loss of a child. For many, it is a story that must be told. All they need is a listening ear to share with someone, anyone, of how they had to endure the loss of their child. Regardless of the child's age, whether an infant or an adult, the pain does not go away easily.

There are many "do's and don'ts" when talking to someone regarding the death of their child. In the article on relationships, loss and grief, Samantha Hayward says, "The soul destroying grief of your child dying is only truly known and understood by those who have endured it" (2016). She also shares a list of things that a grieving parent does not want to hear.

As I conclude our story, Shirley and I will be praying for our readers, your families, your children, and your healing. The loss of a loved one is never easy, but is made especially difficult when it is your child. In my case, part of the healing has come through sharing our story. Allow me to encourage you. Should you be looking at an empty quiver in your life, continue to trust God. Perhaps your quiver will be filled by way of a miraculous healing or maybe your arrows (i.e., children) are ones that have been discarded by others who could not handle the responsibility. Whatever the case, keep your faith through the process.

And to those women or men who choose not to have a child, that too is an individual choice. Know you are special and God has a purpose for you. One great person who comes to mind is Mother Teresa. She was a woman who chose to take a different course in life. So, if you're someone who chooses to take a different course in life, other than becoming a mother or father, pursue the presence of God and as the scripture tells us, "Trust in the Lord with all thine heart; and lean not unto thine own understanding. In all thy ways acknowledge him, and he shall direct thy paths."

Since our loss, and after overcoming the process of our journey, Shirley and I have been able to minister to countless others about our experience and to share with them the love and mercies of God. I encourage anyone reading this book that if you know of someone who has suffered a loss, the greatest thing you can do for him or her is listen. If you do not know what to say but want to reach out to help them, I have composed a list of support groups and links that provide information you might find helpful. Refer them to any of the following:

Bereaved Parents of the USA
www.bereavedparentsusa.org

Bereavement Services, St Vincent Health
griefHaven - Providing Resources to Parents and Others who have ...
www.griefhaven.org

Bereaved Parent Support Groups - Connect2Help Community...
www.referweb.net

The Compassionate Friends Non-Profit Organization for Grief
www.compassionatefriends.org

Willow House - Grief Support Services
www.willowhouse.org

www.childbereavement.org
www.forums.grieving.com
www.healgrief.org
www.nottheendbook.com
www.stvincent.org/Healthcare-Services/Hospice/Bereavement-Services

References

American Pregnancy Association. (2015) Risks of a cesarean procedure: Cesarean Procedure: Risks & Complications for Mother & Baby. Retrieved from: http://americanpregnancy.org/labor-and-birth/cesarean-risks/

Bears of Hope Pregnancy & Infant loss support Inc. (2016) Arranging Your Baby's Funeral. Retrieved from: http://www.bearsofhope.org.au/a/24.html. Grief Responses of Spouses Following the Death of a Child: A Longitudinal Study. Retrieved from: https://eric.ed.gov/?id=EJ426792

Bohannon J. (1990-91) *Omega: Journal of Death and Dying*, v22 n2 p109-21.

Bryon J. (2011) The Biblical World, Dedicated to the study of all things biblical. Infertility and the Bible 2: The Defective Wife: Retrieved from: http://thebiblicalworld.blogspot.com/2011/01/childlessness-and-bible-2-defective.html

Center for Disease Control and Prevention. (2015) About Premature Birth

Frank, Jan. (1995). Door of Hope, recognizing and resolving the pains of your past. Published in Nashville TN. By Thomas Nelson, Inc.

Demary ED. (1985) How Are You Praying? A Manual on the Practice of Prayer. Franscis Asbury Press of Zondervan Publishing House. Grand Rapids. MI

Fuller M. (2002) Building Materials for Life. Macon GA.: Smyth & Helwys Publishing

Galica, Jean., (n.d). The Effects of the death of a child on a Marriage. Retrieved from: http://www.theravive.com/research/The-Effects-of-the-Death-of-a-Child-on-a-Marriage

Grief Loss Recovery Hope and Health through Creative Grieving. (n.d.). In Recovery-from-grief. Retrieved from http://www.recover-from-grief.com/

Hawkins K. (2015) Christian CrierTop Seven Verses about Barren Women. Retrieved from: http://www.patheos.com/blogs/christiancrier/2015/08/14/top-7-bible-verses-about-barren-women/

Hayward S. (2016) How to talk to a parent who is in grief. From someone who's been there. Retrieved from: http://www.mamamia.com.au/ten-points-i-wish-every-person-knew-about-the-death-of-a-child/

Kanai M, Ashida T, Ohira S, Osada R, Konishi I. (2008) A new technique using a rubber balloon in emergency second-trimester cerclage for fetal membrane prolapse. *Journal of Obstetrics & Gynecology Research*, 34(6), 935-940. doi:10.1111/j.1447-0756.2008. 00805. X

Maxwell JC. (2003) Attitude 101: What every leader needs to know. Nashville TN: Thomas Nelson Publishing

Mayo Foundation for Medical Education and Research, (2016) Incompetent Cervix, Disease and Conditions, http://www.mayoclinic.org/diseases-conditions/incompetent-Cervix/basics/definition/con-20035375

Mayo Foundation for Medical Education and Research, (2016) Cervical Cerclage, test and procedures, http://www.mayoclinic.org/tests-procedures/cervical-cerclage/basics/definition/prc-20012949

McDowell J. (1984) His Image...My Image (San Bernardino, CA: Here's Life Publishers, Inc. 31.)

Miller AM. (2016) US News & World Report. Why can't I get pregnant? Retrieved from: http://health.usnews.com/wellness/slideshows/why-cant-i-get-pregnant

Mollette G. (2000) Silent Struggler: A caregiver's Personal Story. Newburgh, IN: A division of GMA Publishing

National Survey of Family Growth, Centers for Disease Control and Prevention [CDC] (2006-2010)

Rainey D, Rainey B. (1998) Family Life, Hope for today Hope for tomorrow, Crafting God's Arrows, a biblical battle plan for parenting. Retrieved from: http://www.familylife.com/articles/topics/parenting/essentials/releasing-your-child/crafting-gods-arrows

Roberts G. (2014) Finding a place for love after the death of a child. Grief Matters: The Australian Journal of Grief & Bereavement, 17(1), 23

Rogers CH, Floyd FJ, Seltzer MM, Greenberg J, Jinkuk H. (2008) Long-Term Effects of the Death of a Child on Parents' Adjustment in Midlife. *Journal of Family Psychology,* 22(2), 203-211. doi:10.1037/0893-3200.22.2.203

Shugerman, (n. d). percentage of married couples who cheat, Catalogs.com info library: Retrieved from http://www.catalogs.com/info/relationships/percentage-of-married-couples-who-cheat-on-each-ot.html

The True Story of "The Crying Indian" (n.d.) Pollution: it's a crying shame. Retrieved from: https://priceonomics.com/the-true-story-of-the-crying-indian/

U.S. Census Bureau and the Centers for Disease Control

Walton JH. (2007) Compassionate Care: An Inspirational Guide for Caregivers of The Seriously Ill.: United States of America. Xulon Press

Weiss MF. (n.d.) Grieving the Loss of a Child. Retrieved: http://www.aamft.org/iMIS15/AAMFT/Content/consumer_updates/grieving_the_loss_of_a_child.aspx

World Health Organization. (2015) Why do so many women still die in pregnancy or childbirth?

About the Author

Having served for over 35 years in ministry, Anthony Walton, PhD is passionately dedicated to supporting and encouraging diverse groups of people in various life situations. His personal story, which is told in this book, coupled with his vast experience in assisting others over the years, gives him a unique ability to inspire others to manage and overcome both spiritual and personal life challenges. He has years of experience in Christian counseling, including both a Doctorate of Philosophy and a Master's degree in this field. Bishop Walton will soon complete a second Master's degree in Marriage and Family Therapy. His occupational background as a Suicide Intervention Counselor also provides him with an insider's look into how to best meet the needs of those who experience discouragement and hardships. Having ministered locally and around the world in such countries as the West Indies, the Dominican Republic, the Bahamas, and West Africa, he understands that compassion happens on many levels. His view is that often times, our personal testimony, no matter how difficult it may be to tell it, could be the very thing that encourages someone to move from pain and loss to hope and victory.

www.ingramcontent.com/pod-product-compliance
Lightning Source LLC
Chambersburg PA
CBHW071850230426
43671CB00012B/2137